Costume Reference 2
Tudors and Elizabethans

MARION SICHEL

Publishers   PLAYS, INC.   *Boston*

First published 1977
© text and illustrations 1977, Marion Sichel

First American edition published by Plays, Inc. 1977

Library of Congress Cataloging in Publication Data

Sichel, Marion
  Costume Reference.
    Includes bibliographies and indexes.
CONTENTS: v. 1 Roman Britain and the Middle Ages –
v. 2. Tudors and Elizabethans
1. Costume – Great Britain – History.
I. Title
GT 730.S48   1977   391'.00941
76-54466   0-8238-0212-4 (vol. 2)

Printed in Great Britain

Contents

Survey

In the Tudor period the long, low squarish buildings seemed to be repeated in the horizontal lines of the costumes. Shoes became more square toed, and ladies' headdresses flatter. The black and white buildings seem to be reflected also in the more sombre colouring of clothes. In Spain black velvet and white linen were much worn, and this became fashionable in England.

New ideas in fashion occurred in a period when the pioneers of trade with Flanders, the Baltic and the Mediterranean countries exposed England to many different influences. They took with them materials and wools and returned with new ideas, jewels and richly coloured expensive materials, all of which influenced the new styles.

From the reign of Edward VI (1547–1553) the bodice and skirt of a dress were separate, with the bodice waist pointed in front and the skirt or kirtle still worn with the Spanish *farthingale*. The influence of Spanish fashion was more than the mere whim of fashionable trends for it had a great political basis. The powerful position of the Spanish Empire under Charles V who ruled over Germany, Austria, the Netherlands and had vast possessions both in South America and Africa, made Spain the most powerful nation in the world. Spanish fashion had to be accepted in the subjugated countries. The marriage in 1554 of Philip II, son of Charles V, who succeeded his father in Spain, Burgundy and the Netherlands, to Mary Tudor, Queen of England, brought about an increase of Spanish dress influence in England.

The progressive and reformatory movements which had started in the early Renaissance period were now being ruthlessly suppressed in the countries over which the mighty Hapsburgs reigned. The difference between the dress of the ordinary people and that of the Court which earlier had diminished, again reasserted more strongly than ever and the gulf between common and courtly dress was enormous.

Dress in the Elizabethan period was the most lavish in English history. Like Henry VIII, Queen Elizabeth was very fond of opulent clothes and jewels, and this was copied by the Court. Costume did not alter very much until 1580, and then the main change was that very wide sleeves were replaced by a tight-fitting style with puffed shoulders, as well as a bishop sleeve and padded rolls extending from the shoulders. In c.1580 the silhouettes of the upper classes showed a long close-fitting bodice with a smooth jewelled and stiffened *stomacher*, enormous padded trunk sleeves and wide hips. An immense circular or fan-shaped ruff framed the face which emerged from the sides and low-backed neckline. Also popular was a wired and lace collar known as a *rebato*. Hair was worn high, being frizzed and curled.

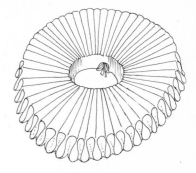

Cartwheel ruff

The period of the second half of the sixteenth century reflects all the heavy, artificial splendour of the Spanish fashion. The functional purpose of the costume was of little importance; what mattered most was the decorative effect. The stiff dark materials were the fashionable image of the period, a background for the encrusted jewels with which many of the dresses were decorated was also a sign of the wealth of the wearer. The human body inside these costumes was subjected to a confusion of torturous aids; nothing was natural or simple: shoulders, waists, stomachs and hips were constricted, corseted, padded, wired, bejewelled and distorted, moulded into man's fashionable style. The hair was shaved, or dyed in a variety of hues, fluffed, curled and likewise bejewelled. Faces were painted and patched. The fashionable mode of the period was the dark-coloured uncomfortable costume with a high stiff, starched collar. The introduction of starch in 1564 caused the ruffs to become even larger and stiffer, reaching ridiculous proportions and aptly called 'millstones'.

The Englishman, William Lee, invented the first knitting machine for stockings in 1589. He was established in Rouen in France and patronized by Henri IV of France. This was an era of great richness and overdressing with many regulations related to dress. For example it was not permitted to wear crimson unless of royal blood, and further, the middle classes

Gentleman Hawk Hunting

were allowed the use of velvet for sleeves only. The *baldrick*, or shoulder sash of satin, was the fashionable wear for both male and female, but a white sash was worn only by the king. The wearing of coloured fur was reserved for the upper classes and black was permitted for the lower order. In this period England began to import Spanish and Italian lace, and both men and women began to adorn their clothes with this costly material. Also introduced into England about this time was perfumed leather in the form of the short Spanish cape and gloves; although worn in several European countries for some time, at the Court of Henry VIII, it only became fashionable towards the end of the sixteenth century. The perfumed gloves were made of satin and velvet fringed with gold, silver or silk and worn by women at Court as well as the men. These were known as *frangipani gloves*.

To a small extent country people followed the Spanish fashion, or as much of it as they were allowed to adopt. Whilst the legs of the peasant and poor women were covered, a low décolletage was sometimes worn, but on the whole the dress of the ordinary people was both lighter in colour and considerably simpler than the dress of the nobility. White collar and cuffs were worn, but without lace trimmings.

Children still wore at this period smaller versions of their elders' clothes.

The decline of Spanish fashion came as northern European countries began to lift the Spanish yoke; France being the first country to lighten the stiff, unbending dignity of Spanish costume and introducing a variance of colour and style, with a great deal of extravagance, breaking away completely from the old styles of farthingales, padding, stiff starched ruffles and tight waists. She remained alone in her new-found freedom of dress for several years the Spanish style continued to be worn generally throughout Europe, the heavy materials and encrusted ornaments that had decorated the gowns and suits in the sixteenth century seemed too expensive both in jewels and material to be cast off so quickly.

Spanish influence was now evolving into a definite style. There was the doublet close-fitting with a short skirt, tight waisted and pointed in front. The *peascod body* which followed the Dutch fashion was an excessively padded long-pointed projecting front, which overhung the girdle. In England this fashion was less extreme. The doublet was fitted with a standing collar often edged with stiffened tabs, standing out at right angles. The tabs or *pickadils* were used to support the earlier small ruffs. In the 1570s the collar became high at the back and low in the front to accommodate the larger ruffs. The fastenings of the doublet ran from the collar to the waist by a series of buttons and loops. The doublet body was stiffened with buckram and well padded with wool, horsehair or any stiffening available. The skirts of the doublet varied from the very short, virtually hidden by the girdle; flared, standing out to cover the join between doublet and the stuffed hose, to a separate scalloped border slit into tabs. Double skirts were not uncommon, the overshirt being shorter than the underskirt. Sleeves were made generally detachable being fastened at the armhole by buttons and the join at the shoulder hidden by 'wings'. These wings were made of the same material as the doublet and worn throughout the period. The sleeves were made either narrow and close-fitting to the wrist, fastening with up to a dozen buttons, or leg-of-mutton shape known as 'trunk' sleeves which were pinked and slashed, usually worn about the 1570s with false hanging sleeves. The wider sleeves were always padded and stiffened, *bombast* being the name given to all types of stuffing so characteristic of the costume of the period.

Hip length fashionable cloak

Girdles were made from either leather, gold, silver, silk or velvet and decorations ranged from embossed leather with hangers to support either a sword or dagger, to precious and semi-precious stones.

Jerkins, or jackets, were usually unpadded and worn over the doublet and fitted with either a low or high standing collar, fastening from collar to waist. The skirt was either short and followed the contours of the doublet, or was long almost reaching the bottom of the hose. The jerkin was worn frequently without sleeves, sometimes with only a short puff sleeve with or without the real or false hanging sleeves. In the 1580s it was considered very fashionable to wear just one sleeve of the jerkin and to leave the other hanging loosely. The 'buff jerkin' or leather jerkin made from oiled ox-hide was in reality a military fashion adapted for civilian fashion.

The gown, which had been in fashion since about the middle of the fifteenth century (see Vol. I), was now used mainly in ceremonial and professional occupations or by the elder men for warmth over the doublet or, by women, as a negligée at home.

Cloaks and capes were the height of fashion until the

Leather jerkin which was worn over doublet

Short Spanish type cape

Trunk hose with canions

beginning of the seventeenth century. A short Spanish cape was the most popular, fitted with a hood, usually deep and pointed, trimmed with buttons and loops, it also had a small turn-down collar. Due to the short length of this cape it could be worn either over one or both shoulders. The French cloak, *manteau à la neitre*, was long, reaching the ankles, and very full, an ideal garment for travelling. The Dutch cloak was again short and full, about waist length, fitted with wide sleeves. The cloak or cape was an essential part of the fashionable male costume and was considered to be a mark of social superiority and frequently was worn even in the home.

A military garment turned into civilian fashion was the *mandilion*, a loosely fitting hip-length jacket with hanging sleeves with wings. The vertical side slits made a back and front panel which were pulled on over the head and buttoned from the standing collar to the chest only. The mandilion was sometimes worn rather strangely in a sideways fashion with the panels draped over the shoulders, and the sleeves hanging down, back and front.

The most characteristic fashion of this period was the ruff. The small ruff, either attached to the shirt or separate, was frequently worn open at the throat. The *medium ruff* was closed all round. The *cartwheel ruff* was large and closed all round. To support the latter was the *underpropper* or *supportasse*, a wire framework attached to the doublet collar with the ruff pinned to it. From the simple goffered band the ruff grew to include double, treble or even more layers, becoming more complex with the introduction of starch in the 1560s. Poking sticks were used to create the tubular pleats.

The term 'hose' was used to indicate breeches. *Trunk hose* were the popular garments of the period, padded and covering the thighs, and in one with the stockings; later the term referred only to the breeches part. The two styles were usually slashed and from the slashing a contrasting colour was visible. *Canions* or leg coverings fitting in the space between the trunk hose and the stockings were also worn. The German trunk hose or *pluderhose* were popular from about mid-century and had large slashings profusely stuffed with coloured silks spilling over the edges. They were usually knee length, but often longer.

Breeches with separate stockings came in various styles. *Venetian*, which fastened just below the knee, were either skin tight with the stockings pulled up over them and gartered above the knee, or gathered in at the waist and

padded round the hips. Popular was the 'Venetian voluminous' type with the pickadil border at the knees. The terms
used were many and varied, such as trunk slops, trunks, etc.
(the word 'slops' meaning usually 'without padding').

Tailored stockings were popular until the end of the
sixteenth century, thereafter knitted stockings became the
vogue. Garters of silk ribbon and taffeta trimmed with
diamonds and jewels of all descriptions were usually tied just
under the knee, holding the stockings in place. Plain buckled
straps were worn and fastened just below the knee with the
stockings rolled back thus completely hiding the strap. The
stockings were clocked in various patterns.

Men's shoes were usually round-toed, with low wedge
heels making an appearance towards the end of the century.
The high heel of the low-cut shoe decorated with a large shoe
rose was only for the ultra-fashionable. Shoes were made
close to the ankle with the upper long and ending in two
small tongues, these were often fastened with straps, or sometimes with thread through an eyelet hole. The uppers were
usually slashed or pinked into a design. Pumps were worn at
this time by both sexes. The high dress boots for riding in the
late 1580s were turned down to just below the knee, the tops
being scalloped. After 1590 they became popular walking
boots. Leggings called *cockers* were made to protect the
stockings.

Hats were now worn both in and out of doors. The flat
hat, a small round beret type with a narrow brim, decorated
with a feather, was popular until about the 1570s. As the
century progressed crowns became higher like a high-
crowned bowler, and all hats whether high, low or flat
crowned were made in leather, beaver, velvet or felt and
often trimmed with ribbon bands, or with gold, silver, pearl
or crystal buttons, and decorated with feathers.

During Elizabeth I's reign (1558–1603), hair was short, and
in the early part of the reign was brushed forward over the
forehead and sides of the face. After 1560 the Italian curly
style as well as the Spanish brushed-back mode became
popular. The short hair-styles of the men and the elaborate
hair-styles of the ladies were very practical when worn
with starched and pleated ruffs. Hair-styles followed a
fashionable mode with the hair being cropped all over, then
brushed up away from the forehead and stuck with the aid
of gum, as also was the moustache and cropped beard, a
fashion which lasted until the end of the sixteenth century.

Men's slashed leather hat

Man wearing bonnet

Fringed glove

From about the 1590s came longer hair-styles reaching the shoulders. The love-lock, a tress of hair very long and plaited with a ribbon tied at the end, was brought forward to hang over the chest and became very fashionable. The wearing of beards was popular throughout the period, the *vandyke, pickdevant, spade beard, square* and *marquistette* are but a few of the types worn. Wigs, patches and make-up were worn only by the dandies of the period.

Elbow-length gauntlet gloves of silk, velvet and gold fringed were often slashed at the fingers to reveal the rings worn. The wearing of one glove while carrying the other was practised throughout as a modish 'trend'. Perfumed gloves imported from France and Spain were fashionable as were doeskin ones for riding.

Handkerchiefs, still a luxury, were usually carried in the hand; made of cambric, lawn, silk or velvet they were trimmed with lace.

Men carried leather or silk purses slung from the girdle from which hung a sword supported by hangers. The dagger was slung in a horizontal position behind the right hip. A gorget or military steel collar was frequently worn as part of civilian fashion.

With the coronation of Queen Elizabeth in 1559 at the age of 25, a new era of fashion came into being. Fashions became more lavish with elaborate embroidery, large ruffs, lighter, padded clothes and brightly coloured materials. The feminine fashions became a combination of these characteristics. Women wore the corseted bodice, which was extremely rigid and stiffened with wooden or whale-bone stays. The waist was low and deeply pointed in front, and up to about the 1580s was often scallop-edged. The bodice was probably fastened down the left side by hooks. The neck line could be either low or high; if low it was square cut and arched slightly over the bosom. The low décolletage was covered either by a high-necked chemise with a standing collar and small open frill at the throat, or just with jewellery. The high neck line also had a standing collar with a small medici collar. After about 1580 a closed cartwheel-type ruff was usually worn. The cuffs at the wrist and other decorations matched the collar, these being either hand ruffs or turn-back cuffs, made in the same material as the neck ruff such as lawn, cambric or lace.

Sleeves were close-fitting to the wrist, slightly padded, puffed and slashed, finishing with either the hand ruff or turn-back cuffs. The variation of sleeves included slashed roll wings, double or single or even a large plain roll, with hanging sleeves which, after mid-century were often sham. There was the close-fitting 'gathered' sleeve, being drawn in by many bands up the arm, the 'bishop' sleeve which was full from the shoulder to the wrist, ending with a tight cuff.

The long skirts of wealthy ladies were usually encrusted with precious metal and stones and sometimes worn open to reveal the rich undergown or petticoat of the same length beneath. This was of a conical shape supported by a similar shaped undergown of some stiffened material, the forerunner of the crinoline. The Spanish farthingale (also known as a verdingale) was in vogue from about 1545–1590. It was an undergown spreading out straight from the waist with circular hoops of wood, steel or whalebone. The shape varied from being a funnel, bell-shaped or dome skirt. It was made from canvas, buckram or heavy linen. The overskirt was made to stand stiffly outwards from the waist to the ground, making a smooth surface without any draperies or folds.

The French farthingale became the Court fashion proper about 1580 and lasted well into the 1620s. There were two styles: the 'roll farthingales' known affectionately as the 'bum roll' (a padded bolster roll which was worn round the hips tilted slightly up at the back and tied with tapes in the front) and the 'wheel farthingale' or 'Catherine wheel farthingale' sometimes called the 'Italian' farthingale, which as its name implies was a wheel-shaped structure made from steel or whalebone, usually covered in a damask material. Worn around the waist it had a tilt forward, a raised-up behind, resembling by the turn of the century, as the tilt increased, a large bustle. The skirt was made full enough to be carried out at right angles, falling over the farthingale, then dropping vertically to the feet.

The popular gown which was used for formal occasions and for warmth, was worn over the bodice and skirt. The loose-bodied style, which had fitted shoulders and fell in folds giving an inverted V shape, was opened down the front to reveal the dress beneath and had a standing collar, open at the throat, fitted sometimes with ties which closed the gown from neck to hem. The sleeves were short and puffed out with a kick-up effect at the shoulder, and ended just above the elbow. Fitchets were vertical placket holes which often decorated the gown, and through which articles suspended on the girdle of the skirt could be reached. Popular among

Spanish farthingale worn under the dress

*Peasant woman with face
covering*

the maiden ladies was the Catherine de Medici style of
very low décolletage, which bared the bosom. It is said
that Elizabeth of England wore this style in her later years.

Stockings at this period were either tailor-made or knitted.
Silk stockings were worn by the rich, and it is stated that
Queen Elizabeth was the first English-woman to wear them.
Embroidered garters were also worn, tied just below the
knee. It was in this era that the low-cut shoe with a high heel
first appeared and 'pumps' became very popular. The shoes
had cork soles with both leather and embroidered velvet for
the uppers; worn over the shoes when outdoors were a variety
of overshoes such as *chopines*, clogs or pattens and *pantoffles*.
Pantoffles, a type of overshoe, were slipper-like without a
back, made of leather with cork platform soles, worn over
boots on the bad roads. White leather was popular for
women as were lightweight shoes made of deer, goat and
sheepskin.

Gimped slashes without a base decorated the vamps, with
uppers cut in three pieces joined at the back and sides. Very
rarely were they made in two pieces without the back piece
as they were ill-fitting. Soles were always separate and sewn
to the finished shoe.

The first heels were seen in Queen Elizabeth's reign, and
were $3\frac{1}{2}$–4cm high. At first people found them uncomfortable and their calves swelled. This was due to the un-
accustomed height as well as the incorrect positioning of the
heels. Chopines were from 10–17cm in height whilst pattens
had wooden or cork soles, and pantoffles had cork soles
but with the front uppers only. The fronts of the shoes
became higher until eventually they were known as
'tongues'.

Brocade was a very popular material for ladies' shoes as
were all embroidered materials and the most fashionable
colours in this period were russet, saffron, black, white, red,
green, blue, pink and yellow. Stockings were also made in
all these colours and were now better fitting.

Feminine hats followed the men's style with brims and
feathers, but were generally smaller and worn fairly straight
on the head, usually over a linen cap. A popular style of
bonnet was the 'Mary Stuart hood' made of lawn, cambric
or linen trimmed with lace, its particular feature being the
dip of the front border, which was wired to form a curve
over the centre of the forehead. Bonnets such as the French
hood or *bongrace*, the *cornet*, the *taffeta pipkin*, the *lettice cap*

were also worn. Hats for riding and travelling became popular towards the end of the century. These were of various shapes and materials from felt to beaver. Other head-wear during this period was in the way of simple head coverings resembling hair nets known as *reticulated cauls*, covering the back of the head, made from silk or hair. The forehead cloth was a triangular piece of material, with the point at the back, the straight edge round the forehead and tied under the chin, these were worn with coifs, cauls and neckerchiefs. Resembling a large calash was the arched hood made from a thick material wired along one border, which was bent into a curve to create an arch shape over the head but projected forward over the forehead.

Coif hood

The wire supports were either fixed to the shoulders or sometimes as low as the waist. The drapery could be gathered at the back of the neck or the waist, or was allowed to hang freely in various lengths down the back. It was not considered incorrect for ladies to walk bare-headed, or with just head ornamentations.

Throughout the period women wore long hair plaited or coiled behind the head, usually hidden by the headdress, the front hair was always worn away from the forehead, but in various styles. If a centre parting was used the hair was waved and bunched out at the sides, or turned back over pads giving fullness at the temples. Without a parting the hair was pulled over a *palisadoe* or wire frame which dipped in the centre like a 'widow's peak' widening at the sides. False hair, ornamented dressed wigs, feathers and dyed hair were very much in vogue. The colours red and blonde in the dyed hair being most popular, and as Elizabeth set the fashion of the English Court, red dyed hair was a direct compliment to her.

Powder and rouge were used, and patches made of silk and velvet in various shapes and sizes were applied to the face by means of mastic (glue). Pale complexions remained in vogue, and white powder, with a hint of rouge on the cheeks was used very occasionally. Make-up was not in general use until the reign of Queen Elizabeth, headdresses such as the gable and French hood protecting the face against the weather.

Perfumes, however, were popular, the majority being imported, whilst some scents were made of herbs in England. *Pomanders*, introduced into England *c.* 1500, were generally attached to the ends of a girdle or worn on a chain around the neck. They contained scents and herbs. The pomander was

Gloved hand with ribbon points holding handkerchief

often made of gold or silver filigree in the shape of an apple, the word 'pomander' being from the French *pomme d'ambre*. Gentlemen often carried hollowed-out oranges, containing scents or herbs.

By 1559 cosmetics were in general use and a popular fashion was the use of white powder as foundation, with rouge being added to the cheeks. A kind of lipstick was made of ground alabaster or plaster of paris, combined with a colouring ingredient, mixed into a paste and formed into a pencil shape and allowed to dry. All these cosmetics contained a certain amount of lead which was very injurious to the skin and gave rise to skin-diseases. Eyelids and even teeth were tinted.

To preserve the make-up the face was covered with a thin layer of egg-white, and to protect the face even more thoroughly, masks were worn. These were cut in an oval shape with openings for the eyes and were held in place with a button grasped between the teeth. Hands were also considered necessarily to be white.

Soap, although popular, being imported from Castille in Spain and from Italy, was not used to a great extent.

As the wearing of headdresses diminished and elaborate hair-styles became popular, hair had to be well kept. A medieval habit of plucking the eyebrows and hair from the forehead continued throughout the Tudor and Elizabethan eras. As Queen Elizabeth's hair got thinner and lost its lustre, she wore wigs, which, inevitably, increased their popularity with the wealthier classes.

Accessories for the costume varied – but mainly consisted of gloves, handkerchiefs, ruffs, bags and fans. Scarves and mufflers were worn, the former for show made from silk and tasselled in gold or silver, the latter for warmth made from taffeta or velvet. Muffs were carried, being small and tubular, made in fur and silk, and were usually slung from the girdle.

Under the Tudors
(1485–1545)

The fashions of the Middle Ages were now gradually changing with the coming of the Renaissance to England. Under the reign of the House of Tudor a whole vista of changes were taking place with the removal of the old regime of aristocracy in the Wars of the Roses. These also affected fashion. With the first of the four Tudor monarchs, Henry VII (1485–1509) the medieval mode of fashion remained more or less as before, under the influence of the French and Italian, but new styles, from the brevity of the male costume to that of a more excessive and extravagant style of dress began to emerge.

Male costume

DOUBLET

The doublet (1450–1670) remained close fitting to the waist and reached down to just cover the hips. It was lined with quilted padding and sewn in such a way that the stitch lines were not readily seen. From 1485 the doublet could be worn with or without a skirt, but from 1530 the skirt was always attached. The skirts when worn were either full, falling over the hips or were short and narrow being tabbed or scalloped. A girdle was sometimes worn but very popular was a small sash knotted in front.

The front of the doublet was closed with hooks and eyes, buttons or lacing. The neckline was a standing collar with a V-shape cut away in front during the period 1450–1490, but between 1490–1530 it was collarless with a deep square neckline or a fairly low V-shape in front, this being tied loosely

Children wore the same styles and fashions as their elders. This boy is wearing a slashed, padded doublet and trunk hose with a cod piece. The shoes matched the slashings of the costume (c.1545).

Slouched and slashed brimmed bonnet. Low square-necked doublet with open jacket and full to the elbow sleeves (c.1517).

with lacing. Between 1490–1520 in place of lacing, the opening was covered by the shirt alone or by a stomacher, a *partlet* or a *plackard*. These last three were separate pieces, usually made of a brocaded material often matching the detachable sleeves. From 1500–1536 the neck-line became oval in shape and later, from 1530–1540, fitted closer round the neck.

The sleeves of the doublet in the period 1450–1500 were close fitting to the wrist then full to the armhole where they were attached by lacing or points, the join-line concealed by the overmantle or a hanging sleeve. This was even more common after 1540. The detachable sleeve followed the ordinary sleeve styles which varied from being close-fitting to being full at the shoulders and elbow. The wide full sleeve was panned from the elbow to the shoulder. The slashed sleeve was also full and wide-fitting close to the wrist, the slashings revealed the shirt or lining which was usually of a contrasting colour. Sometimes the waistcoat sleeve was revealed.

Slashings were popular at elbow level, later to be increased with a further slashing higher up the arm. Later a number of small slashes running down the length of the arm became very fashionable. Popular was the long slash which revealed the shirt from the wrist to the elbow. Between 1500–1580 the wearing of the two-sleeve fashion was very common. The doublet sleeve was not actually worn but hung loose and became just a sham sleeve. The sleeve which was worn was usually of the detachable type and in contrasting material and colour to the costume; this sleeve, which was partially hidden, was known as a 'half sleeve' or 'fore sleeve'. The sleeves were close to the wrist and slipped on over the hand, either through an aperture wide enough to take the hand or by a small vertical slit which was closed with buttons.

Round the waist of the body of the doublet were eyelet holes grouped in pairs which matched similar eyelet holes round the waist of the hose. Through these holes were threaded ties or 'points', which were tied into bows, thus supporting the hose. These points were either concealed on the underside of the doublet or under the long skirts but it was also common to see them tied outside. The wealthier classes had the points tipped with decorative metal tags or 'aiglets', the poorer people wore leather or cord points. The doublet materials for the fashionable were silks, satins, velvet, damask, rich cloths of gold, whilst woollen cloths were worn by the less wealthy and the poor people.

SHIRT

The shirt, usually of linen and usually white, was very full and the fullness was gathered onto a narrow band at the low neck-line into pleats and sometimes embroidered in coloured thread. Shirts had always to be visible above the doublet.

Later, in the first quarter of the sixteenth century, the shirt collar became higher and ended with a band closely fitting round the neck. By the 1530s the band was enlarged into a standing collar and further edged with a turn-down collar resembling a frill, this being the forerunner of the ruff. By the 1560s it had reached its maximum height and size. Until the early 1530s the shirt collar was buckled on one side, usually out of sight, this being popular with the deep square neckline. Later buttons, hooks and eyes or lacing closed the front down to the waist. In this period shirt sleeves had frills which began to show below at the wrist of the doublet. The sleeves were gathered in a great fullness both at the shoulder and at the wrist allowing the shirt to be pulled through the slashed doublet sleeves.

JACKETS

The jacket or 'jacquette' was sometimes called a jerkin, although this term did not come into wide use until later but referred to the buff jerkins which were worn at this time. Similar to the doublet which it was worn over, the jacket was high waisted with a close-fitting body and a skirt which varied in length according to the fashionable trend but always covered the doublet. From 1490–1540 the body of the garment had a deep V-shape which came down to the waist in front, the opening being covered-in either by a plackard or simply the doublet. Up to 1510 the V-shape was edged with a rever which came from the waistline in a narrow form then, broadening as it reached the shoulders, continued over the shoulders to make a rounded flat-falling collar at the back. This changed to a square form about 1540.

The jacket was fastened down the front by buttons, lacing, or hooks and eyes or could be left open, the neck being round or square without a collar. In the 1540s a narrow stand-up collar was attached and gradually increased in height similar to the doublet fashion.

During the early part of the century the skirt of the doublet was made in strips of alternating coloured materials giving a striped effect. The skirts were very full and were open down the front, varying in length from just below knee length to

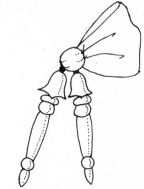

Ribbon loop with points which could be of ivory.

Bonnet with the wide turned-up and slashed brim and soft crown, and a decorative medallion on the side. The slits were trimmed with laces which threaded through the slashes. The bonnet was worn with a sideways tilt. The doublet had a standing collar with the chemise frill visible above. The sleeves were with a slashed design, with the chemise sleeve frills showing at the wrists. The gown had fur edging and a cape collar. An elaborate neck chain was worn (c.1523).

The halo brimmed bonnet was trimmed with ostrich tips. The jacket had a 'U' shaped opening to the waist which revealed the slashed doublet with puffs emerging from the slashings. The skirt was full. A sash girdle and hanger was worn to hold the dagger. The shorter gown sleeves with hanging sleeves behind revealed the decorated sleeves of the doublet. The gown was edged and lined with fur. The square shoes also had a slashed design (c.1539).

hip length, the later fashion being more popular in the 1530s. Skirts worn on horseback were called *bases*, and varied in length to just below knee length or at knee length up to 1518, then above knee length until the 1540s.

Sleeves could be completely absent, long and funnel shaped, puffed and full to the elbow, close fitting to the elbow then close fitting to the wrist and closed with buttons, or just short and puffed to the elbow. The last two styles often had hanging sleeves attached which were usually wide and funnel shaped with openings in various shapes, the most popular being long vertical or horizontal slits placed at different levels from wrist, elbow and shoulder height. The jackets were made in a variety of materials, leather being popular for country gentlemen. Decorations followed the doublet style of slashings.

PETTICOTE

A short coat-like garment falling to waist-length, the petti-cote was worn between the doublet and the shirt. It had a low round shaped neck-line and was worn either with or without sleeves, these often being detachable. The petticote was well padded and undoubtedly used for warmth and always worn with a doublet or indoors as a negligée. Later it became known as the 'waistcoat'. Sometimes the hose were attached to the petticote instead of to the doublet by exactly the same method, with eyelet holes and 'trussing the points' with lacing.

GOWNS

Worn over the doublet or jacquette was the gown, this was built over the shoulders giving a very broad appearance and hanging loosely down in thick folds. The front was usually left open but could, on occasions, be tied round the waist by a girdle, but uncommonly was fastened by points from the neckline to the waist. The bound edges of the front were turned back into revers, which began narrow then gradually broadened out over the shoulders and then, similar to the jacquette, formed a rounded or square falling collar at the back, called a cape. Later the revers remained narrow and formed into a simple rolled collar without the cape. The length of the gown varied from short to knee-length or just above and was known as the 'demi-gown' which was popular for horse riding from 1500–1560s. The 'long-gown' was worn to ankle length for all ceremonial purposes, but

Flat cap decorated with a feather at the side and a medallion at the front. The full-skirted doublet had a low standing collar, revealing the embroidered shirt. From the puffed-out shoulder sleeves of the short gown were visible slashed sleeves. The breeches or upperstocks, were also slashed. The cod piece was prominent. A narrow belt with hangers was worn to hold the dagger and sword. The shoes had round toes and were close to the ankle (c.1540).

most popular was the mid-calf length gown, both for warmth and practicality.

Sleeve fashions varied over the era, from the full turned-back cuff to the long wide funnel variety, forming the hanging sleeve, the arms coming through the slits at the sides (1500–1520s). From about 1530 the large puffed shoulder fashion became popular; this could be worn with or without a hanging sleeve, often attached to a close-fitting sleeve which was tight to the wrist. The gowns were made from cloth, damask, velvets and ornamented with fur.

CLOAK

From *c.*1545 the *Spanish cloak* began to supersede the gown. Made in either a circular or semi-circular form it was fastened by a cord over one shoulder. A short shoulder cape known as a *tippet* was worn with both the gown and the cloak. Over-garments were known by various names such as frock, coat, cassock and gabardine.

LEG COVERING

The leg coverings worn were similar to modern tights. The stockings or *netherstocks* and the breeches or *upperstocks* were joined together. The upperstocks were made up from crossed pieces of materials and decorated with slashes (1500–1515) and after this period gradually became wider and fuller. From this fashion emerged the *trunk-hose* (1540–1560). The breeches became wider increasing from the crotch to mid-thigh, the addition often being panned. The sack-shaped flap which was formed around the crutch and called the cod-piece continued in use during 1515–1575. During this period it became very extended with the use of padding, the extension was slashed matching the other part of the upperstocks. Garters were worn, usually just below the knee, the ends forming a bow on the outside of the leg.

SHOES

Boot-hose or overstockings were worn inside the boots to safeguard the under-hose. They were loose and wide at the top so that they could be turned down to form a broad cuff just below the knee. In the early part of the century shoes were close fitting to the ankle and were again fashionable in the mid-century. Popular among the fashionable nobility was the low-cut shoe which was fastened by a strap across the foot, 1500–1540.

Crude peasant shoe, made of thick leather and fastened with either a bar or lacings.

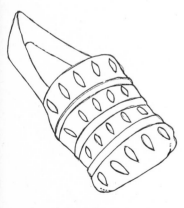

Leather shoe with square toes and bands of contrasting leather with satin visible through the slashes.

Thick cloth shoes were not waterproof and therefore worn with pattens. The shoes could also be made of soft leathers, or for peasants, a thick hide, usually in black.

Weaving, mainly done by women, advanced during the fifteenth and sixteenth centuries, and the materials made were also used for under-shoes, as well as the linings for outdoor ones.

Hooks and buttons were used as shoe fastenings; eyelet holes were mainly just punched into the leather. On the shoes of the wealthier classes these eyelet holes were sewn around in a button-hole stitch.

Shoes became broader, the toes being padded at the sides with moss or hair to make them seem almost as wide as they were long. Slashes were repeated on vamps similar to those on the sleeves which revealed puffs of lace or fine material. The 'duckbilled' toe was square with rounded corners and a central point. Extremely squared shoes became so wide that Henry VIII ordered the width to be limited to 15cm.

Geometrical patterns were popular as decorative slashings. Among the wealthier classes jewels were often sewn on as decoration.

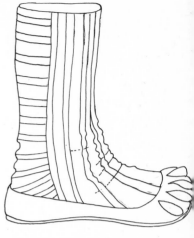

Leather shoes with puffs showing through the slashings at the toes. The striped socks were joined in one with the shoes.

Castellated shoe with coloured satin visible through the slashings.

Soft leather or felt shoe, duckbilled with wide toes and top wing-shaped.

Soft leather or felt boot in a fashionable shape, tied under the knee. The top could either be pulled over the knee or folded back. For the upper classes the lining was in a contrasting colour.

Slashed ankle boot with cuff.

(Right) wide Tudor shoe at its most extreme, with the toes padded with a variety of stuffings to keep the shape.

Bonnet with a slashed, decorated brim and soft, low crown (c.1500).

Bonnet with a wide, slouched and slashed brim (c.1525).

Child wearing low-crowned bonnet with ostrich feather decoration worn over a caul (c.1550).

HEAD-WEAR

The wearing of hats indoors remained in vogue. During the period of 1500–1545 the small bonnet with a variously styled brim was very popular. A wide-brimmed, low-crowned hat which was worn either tilted towards the back of the head or slung over the back suspended with string cords and decorated with large ostrich feathers was popular from the 1490s to the first decade of the sixteenth century. Common throughout the sixteenth century was the small round cap with the turned up brim. Made in four sections it had a low flat crown, round or square, the brim often cut into several pieces, or cut away in the front leaving just side pieces. The later model was that of the buttoned cap from *c.*1520 and continued to be worn throughout the century, not in a stylish way but as a very practical everyday form of headwear. The brim, as in the previous style, was cut away in front and the side pieces could be turned down over the ears like the later balaclava hat, or the sides could be turned up and fastened by a button over the top. Also fashionable was the soft full crown which was pleated onto a headband similar to a large beret. The large brim was turned up and slit at the sides making front and a back pieces. The hat was decorated with a brooch.

Another form of head-wear during this period was the German fashion of the low-crowned, broad-brimmed *barett* which came in many exaggerated forms. The brim was invariably sewn on, consequently the straighter the cut the more the brim hung down. Likewise if it were cut circular the more it stood out horizontally. The brim was either cut into many sections or pleated. Often small triangular pieces were cut out or slashed. The trimmings were remarkable in their inventiveness, coloured laces or ribbons ornamented the brim by being threaded through the incisions and placed into fluted trimmings. Contrasting coloured ribbons adorned the edges. Plumes of pheasant or ostrich feathers in gay colours and aiglets were added as decoration, hat-ties were used to secure the hat under the chin. This style remained popular until the 1530s.

During the 1520s and until the latter part of the century the bonnet was worn with the turned-up brim, 'halo style'. This style of bonnet had a low crown obscured by a deep brim often decorated with ostrich feather tips or with a drooping feather hanging over one side. The fashionable way to wear this type of bonnet was with a sideways tilt and often over a caul. The flat hat, popular from the 1530s to the

1570s, was very plain with a very low crown and a narrow brim with the minimum of decoration, either a small feather or a single medallion, popular with the less wealthy. Undercaps were still worn, the coifs now being worn by the elderly or professional men only. The caul, when worn, was close-fitting and worn at the back of the head and made in very rich threaded materials. The term 'nightcap' applied to both the decorated style worn indoors and to the plain style worn in bed.

HAIR-STYLES

Hair-styles changed considerably over the century. From 1485–1515 the hair was long to the shoulders often with a fringe, the face clean shaven. Lasting until the 1530s was the fashion for hair long to the neck with a forehead fringe with the face now sporting a short moustache and beard. About 1520 short hair became more fashionable, being bobbed to chin level. This style was known as 'polled' and was very popular from about 1550.

After *c.* 1530 to *c.* 1550 beards and moustaches were worn and varied in style. After this time the Spanish-type pointed beard became the mode, as also did the self-explanatory 'spade', 'swallow-tail' and 'round' beards.

Wigs of white or yellow silk were also worn as well as false hair attached to tilted berets. It was also popular to blacken the eyebrows. From the 1530s to the 1540s the hair became shorter, and more common was the trimmed beard both square and round after the French fashion. Until the early seventeenth century the hair remained short with the beards longer and fuller.

Flat cap with a stalk. Hair style was short and bobbed (c.1527).

Flat cap. Hair style was short and a short, trimmed moustache and rounded beard was popular (c.1535).

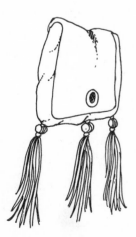

Type of pouch with three hanging tassels (1528–1530).

Flat cap with stalk on top. Short beard and moustache was worn (c.1530).

TOP LEFT: *Low-bodiced gown with partlet 'fill-in' and wide sleeves (c.1540).*
TOP RIGHT: *Large flat 'barett'-style hatwear (c.1527).*

BOTTOM LEFT: *Broad-shouldered gown worn with squared-toed shoes (c.1540).*
BOTTOM RIGHT: *Close-fitting bodice dress with full skirt and gable hood with decorated front lappets (c.1536).*

TOP: *High-necked dress and medici collar (c.1548).*
LEFT: *Fashionable Spanish-style cloak (c.1550).*
RIGHT: *Close-fitting bodice with low décolletage and large sleeves. Spanish farthingale (c.1547).*

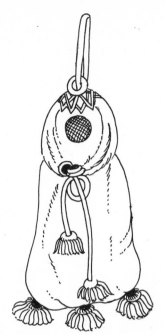

Pouch with tasselled draw-string and three tassels (1528–1530).

Embroidered money pouch which could be suspended from a belt (c.1550s).

ACCESSORIES

Gloves were popular with the wealthier classes. They had short cuffs often of different material and colour from the hand. They were usually slashed as also were the fingers which showed the rings. At Court imported perfumed gloves from Italy were gaining popularity. Mittens were also worn and, like gloves, were made of silks, velvets, satins and various kinds of leather.

Female Costume, 1485–1545

Although the Renaissance had begun prior to 1485 its full significance was felt under the Tudor kings and queens. The dress of women briefly remained medieval in style then gradually changed. A new style of women's dress appeared about 1495 characterized by a fitted square-necked bodice. Above this was visible the top of the kirtle or a neckerchief. The bodice could also be laced across a V-shaped opening to below the waist.

GOWN AND KIRTLE

In the sixteenth century the most typical women's garment was the gown and kirtle. The voluminous gown was the over-garment made in one piece although often joined together at the waist. The kirtle, which was worn over the chemise or nether-garments, could be worn either under the gown or even without the gown. Made with a bodice and skirt, it was joined either by sewing or (very uncommonly) by points. After the mid-century the bodice and skirt were made as separate pieces. The gown during the early part of the century was high-waisted and close-fitting to the figure. The full skirt fell from the hips in heavy folds to the ground with a long train behind. The neck line was low with a square-cut décolletage and a V-shape cut behind and laced across or fastened down the front to the waist, usually by hooks and eyes. The décolletage was covered in by the bodice of either the kirtle or the chemise, whichever was the highest, and often a separate piece of material was folded across the opening forming a V-shape.

The sleeves were usually close fitting from the shoulder, increasing to a wide opening at the wrist where they were turned back into a deep cuff showing a coloured lining or fur. Through the gown sleeve the kirtle sleeve was visible and came to a close fit at the wrist. Sometimes the gown sleeve

French hood decorated with jewels coming to two points either side of the face. The hair had a central parting. The under kirtle had wide sleeves ending with close-fitting frilled cuffs. The full-skirted overgrown was open down the front. A Medici collar was worn with a short necklace and pendant. The close fitting sleeves of the gown ended in wide fur-trimmed cuffs.

was close-fitting, the length of the arm finishing with a wide funnel-shaped cuff open at the back.

The full skirt with its train was often hitched up to the waist and fastened by a brooch, tucked into the waist girdle or carried over one arm, always exposing the coloured lining. The train, however, became less fashionable after the 1540s. The kirtle was usually quite simple, more often than not concealed by the gown. It had a full skirt and was fastened down the front to the waist. The neck-line varied from high to low and from square to round. The sleeves were usually close-fitting to the wrist ending in a small chemise cuff frill or were slashed, with the chemise sleeve being pulled through the slashing.

Dress with a square neckline and close-fitting upper sleeves, the deep cuffs turned back to the elbows. The Spanish farthingale skirt with the inverted 'V' shape exposed the underskirt. The French hood had upper and nether billiments.

After about 1525 the bodice portion of the kirtle became closer fitting and stiffened with a rounded waist and about mid-century the waist line began to dip slightly in the front. The neck-line remained square in front with the décolletage falling to the shoulders with the front edge now slightly arched over the bosom. The décolletage was filled in, in various ways, by heavy jewellery or a high-necked chemise buttoned at the throat with a single button with no edge-to-edge fastening. Sometimes the décolletage opening was covered in by a stomacher or partlet, usually collarless, but by 1530 a narrow stand-up collar was added with a narrow frill, fastening down the front from the neck line.

After about 1525, the kirtle became more elaborate and was

worn on its own. The bodice had a wide square neckline, and formed a V-shape at the back. The edge of the décolletage was richly laced and embroidered with jewels. The skirt was conical in shape and sometimes open in front revealing the underskirt which was of a contrasting colour. A necklace with a pendant was always worn. The chemise worn under the kirtle had a stand-up collar which showed above. Sometimes, however, a separate fill-in or partlet would be worn.

After about 1535 the *Medici collar* – a low stand-up collar revealing the chemise collar or a short necklace – became much favoured.

Up until the mid-century, in the 1560s, both over and under sleeves were worn. The oversleeve was close fitting at the shoulder then distended abruptly at the elbow into a wide opening with a broad turn-back cuff which revealed the contrasting lining or fur, the cuff often being fastened to the upper sleeve. The undersleeves were close fitting to the arm and wrist and often detachable, fastened at the shoulders by points or ties. They could be cut to produce a deep curve from the wrist to the elbow, this lower seam was usually open and fastened together at intervals with aiglets or ribbons, the spaces being filled in by puffs of the chemise pulled through. Without the oversleeve the undersleeve was very full and closed at the wrist with the upper seam left open, the edges embroidered and, similar to the upper or oversleeve, fastened at intervals by jewels or ribbons, with the chemise sleeve drawn through; the wrist ended with the narrow chemise cuff frill.

During the decade 1530–1540 the skirt, which was full and gathered in at the waist, gradually became shorter to ground length and trainless, and at this time also the gored skirt extended to a cone shape without fullness from the narrow waist to the hem and the inverted V-shape at the front revealed the embroidered decorative under-petticoat. A girdle was always worn with this fashion.

After c.1545 the stiff close-fitting bodice dipped into a deep point from the waistline. Popular was the dark contrasting yoke with a low neck-line collar made from a light material with a V-shaped opening down the edge (the Medici collar).

The bodice with side fastening was now worn with both a high- and low-necked chemise which was fitted with a stand-up collar which fastened down the front or was loosely tied with string band cords. Also popular was the low collar, open in the front revealing the high chemise frilled collar.

Early English hood with a semi-circular drapery embroidered on the front edge with a 'clock' ornamentation at the division; undercap and hair were visible.

Gable hood with the lappets pinned up (c.1528).

SHOES AND STOCKINGS

Stockings were usually long to above knee length, tailored, and garters in the form of ties and buckle fastenings were worn. Women's shoes followed very closely those worn by their male counterparts, both pattens and riding buskins being very popular. Shoes were fastened with ornamental buckles or laces and reached the ankle. A lower type (*c.* 1515) similar to a backless mule, returned to fashion with the edges cut in various designs and the vamps in geometric patterns. Decoration was added by means of jewellery.

HEAD–WEAR

Head-wear showed a complete change of style and fashion, the hennin and taller head-gear was now replaced by a very much lower and closer-fitting style. It started as a small crown shape and had a front band which hung down to the sides – an adaptation of the truncated hennin of the 1460s (see Vol. 1). The crown was trimmed with contrasting bands at the intersections of the joins and was known as the bonnet headdress.

Undercaps became very popular and were worn with most headdresses. Hoods, also very common during the early part of the century (1500–1530), were placed over the head and allowed to fall in folds to shoulder length; at either side a slit was inserted to about ear level, this made a curtain effect at the back and two streamers or lappets falling in front, thus framing the face with edges either turned back revealing a contrasting coloured lining or pulled well back showing the under-cap, over this turn-back was usually placed a wide band of embroidery. After about 1515 the curtain at the back and the side streamers or lappets were made much shorter. The *Mary Stuart hood* style (of Flemish origin) was made of a stiffened plain linen and shaped round the face with a slight dip over the forehead, coming down in a curve to just below the cheeks and ending in folds over the shoulders. The *English hood* or *gable headdress* (1500–1540), was similar in cut and style to the hood described with the following difference: the characteristic pointed arch piece which framed the face. This arch form was manufactured by means of a stiffened wire and support framework. Up to *c.*1525 this head-gear had a full draped appearance and was always worn with an undercap and hair just visible. The later version of the English hood was stiffer in form with the falling drapery being considerably reduced. The front

English hood with side lappets turned up to reveal the undercap. The back streamers were allowed to fall loosely. The front hair was concealed in striped rolls (c.1530).

Plain, stiffened hood (c.1530).

Gable hood with lappets (c.1535).

Gable hood with lappets turned up (c.1538).

English hood with the side lappets and back turned up. The rolls on the forehead contained the hair (c.1536).

Gable hood with the back drape replaced by two double strips of material turned up and pinned to the top of the gable. The sides of the undercap became shorter (c.1540).

Flemish style hood built on a stiffened, square-shaped understructure curving forward either side of the face, and covered in a fine embroidered gauze (c.1526).

Bongrace worn over a coif (c.1536).

French hood revealing frilled cap beneath (c.1540).

Flat-crowned French hood with a decorative border called an 'upper billiment' (c.1554).

Large lettice cap (c.1527–1528).

streamers (lappets) were turned up at ear level and fastened by pinning to the top of the crown. The back drapery was replaced by streamers which could also be turned up and pinned to the crown, or if left hanging they fell to almost waist length. The back of the hood was often formed into a flat diamond shape.

The stiff under-cap was still an important base for this style, the side curves were often fastened under the chin with a narrow band. The hair was hidden in rolls which crossed in the centre between the forehead and the gable front, this area being filled in by silk striped padded rolls. Sometimes the hair was twisted spiral fashion and tied with ribbon.

The small stiff based *French hood* (1530–1580) was worn towards the back of the head. The front edge, horse-shoe shaped, was close fitting to the head and curved on either side to just over the ears. The back of the crown was lifted and followed the shaped curve over the head. The hanging drapery behind was either arranged into folds or was a plain piece of material which fell to the shoulders. Stiffened, it could be turned up to lie over the top of the crown with the straight border falling slightly over the forehead, supposedly to shield the skin from the sun's rays, and was called the *bongrace*. The French hood was secured by a band under the chin.

The English version (1525–1558) of the French hood differed in only minor points – it had a straight front edge and the crown was less tilted and projected a little further out over the temples, but remained the same in all other respects. The decorative edges of the French hood were called the *billiment*. The upper billiment decorated the tilted curve at the back of the crown, the nether billiment edged the lower front curve. The billiment could be made from materials such as velvets, satins and silks interwoven with precious stones and often the decorations matched the décolletage or the accessories worn, such as necklaces or girdles.

The accessories to the French hood were the bongrace which was also treated as a separate item, and could be worn alone or with a coif.

The *cornet* (1530–1615) was identical to the bongrace with minor variations of shape, being pointed in front.

Sometimes an undercap was worn with the French hood, the edge of which was visible and either pleated or embroidered. The pleated undercap was visible, as now also was the hair with a centre parting. The front part of the hood had

Flat cap worn over an undercap and embroidered frontlat (1532–1543).

31

a velvet or satin band 5–8cm wide, usually in red, black or white. The back was invariably made of black velvet to replace the characteristic lappets of the gable hood; a piece of double material, either pleated or smooth hung down.

An under-cap was always worn under hats and caps and often wired to a shape. The cap was secured with a pin to the hair or with a strap under the chin. A band or frontlet worn just beneath it could be embroidered or goffered and was just visible.

Although not often worn at this period, hats were flat with a halo-like brim similar to the men's and worn straight with a backward tilt, whereas men wore them at an angle. These hats were usually of velvet and, according to rank, ornamented with gold and jewels, aiglettes or feathers.

A cap, popular from about 1525–1550 but more triangular in shape and made of a fur similar to ermine, was the *lettice cap*. The front edge was curved back to reveal the front of the hair, the sides bending forward. The side pieces later became shorter and the cap became smaller, an undercap or frontlet being worn with it.

HAIR-STYLES

Women's hair-styles remained concealed during this period. With the early hood fashions the hair was barely visible. Later with the gable mode the hair, parted in the centre, was seen under the arch portion. With the advent of the later English variation (1525–1558) it was again completely covered by padded rolls. The French hood displayed more hair from a centre parting, at first sleek and smooth, then from about 1540, waved. The fashion for hair in a long loose flowing style was worn only by young girls, brides and at various ceremonial functions by royal ladies, the hair then being adorned with goldsmith's work, billiments, and flower garlands.

The centre parting with the coils on either side made a secure base for the gable headdress. Occasionally loose hair hung down over the shoulders or down the back beneath the hood. Slightly waved hair was also sometimes visible.

About 1520 the lappets and back-hanging piece of the hood were pinned up and plaited hair, encased in a striped covering brought to the front, was visible beneath the gable, being fastened across the forehead.

Small lettice cap with a frontlet (c.1541).

Large brimless bonnet with undercap and frontlet. A neckerchief could also be worn over the shoulders (c. 1534).

Small brimless bonnet worn over undercap and frontlet. A neckerchief was often worn over the shoulders (c. 1540).

ACCESSORIES

Ladies' wardrobes consisted of many dress accessories which were used to increase the overall effect of wealth and luxury. The girdle which was a popular accessory came in various types, long and narrow with dangling tassels (1500–1535), the buckled trefoil design with the single dangling end and the jewelled chain with the long end which supported a pomander. The short shoulder cape, worn more as decoration than for warmth, and fitted with a narrow Medici collar, was known as the *tippet*.

The neckerchief, a large, usually white square of material folded lengthwise was used as a 'fill in' for the low décolletage or as a shawl. The *rail, head-rail,* and the *night-rail* were also adaptations of the shawl, being worn around the shoulders and over the head. The chemise, decorated round the neck and wrists as well as being used as a pullthrough in the slashed incisions, was fitted with both high and low collars until the 1550s when the high standing collar was replaced by the small separate neck decoration of the ruff.

Female accessories followed the male fashion in handkerchiefs and gloves. Most other accessories were suspended from the girdle belts such as purses, a book of hours, beads, a pomander. Fur stoles were either carried or suspended by a chain from the girdle. Pomander (1500–1590) was a variation of the French word *pomme* (apple) and named after a scent called 'pomme d'ambre'. It was goldsmith's work, made from gold, silver or ivory, jewelled and enamelled and came in a wide variety of shapes ranging from a flat box, circular or square, to a ball-shape, in a fiiligree with many perforations. All contained perfume for both personal and health reasons. It was usually suspended from the girdle by a long chain and hung down in front. Scent was also carried in finger rings and necklaces.

*Middle-class mother and
young son. Boys were dressed
similar to girls until the age of 5
or sometimes later (c.1540).*

34

High Elizabethan (1545–1603)

Male costume

DOUBLET

The doublet, worn over the shirt, was close-fitting with a short skirt, tight waisted and pointed in front. During the period, the point of the doublet became more pointed as the girdlestead (waistband) curved further downwards. The round-waisted fashion appeared during this time but did not gain popularity until 1590–1610. The body of the doublet was stiffened with coarse materials such as buckram or canvas with busks or pasteboard added in front which were covered over with silks, statins or taffeta. It was then padded ('bombasted') with wool, horsehair or tow, and from 1575–1590 had to be padded still further to accommodate the Dutch fashion of the *peascod belly*. This additional padding was placed at the point of the waist to produce a projection to overhang the girdle, and in some instances reached down to the crotch. There could be as much as six pounds of padding stuffed into the doublet body. The standing collar reached a maximum height, to the ears, during the decade between 1560–1570. Later this tended to fall away in the front to allow for the larger ruffs which tilted towards the front. The collar was fitted with small stiffened tabs (*pickadils*) which spread out sideways at right angles. Although the pickadils could be worn as an ornamental edging they did in fact support the smaller ruffs much worn at this time. Sometimes a narrow collar with a small V-shape opening slit in front was favoured.

The doublet was closed down the front by various fastenings, most commonly by buttons (sewn very closely together) and button-holes (often substituted by loops). Hooks and eyes were also used, these being sewn on the inside edge making them invisible when the doublet was closed.

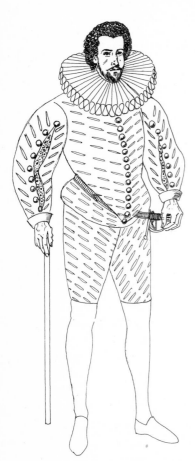

Doublet with peascod belly and matching venetians. Large cartwheel ruff (c.1588).

Doublet buttoned down the front and worn with shoulder wings and matching trunk hose. The ruff and falling band were worn together.

The skirt was short and varied in style to meet the fashion of the moment. During 1575–1585 it was reduced to a very narrow hem edge almost concealed by the waist girdle. Sometimes it stood out in a flare and hid the points which joined the hose to the doublet. The design of the skirt varied with fashionable whims from being plain or slit into inverted V-shapes. Sometimes the tabs or pickadils, overlapped or met edge-to-edge. Occasionally double skirts were worn, the upper portion being narrower than the underskirt. The sleeves of the doublet were worn in most cases with 'wings' (1545–1640) – stiff welt seams which were placed and sewn round the armhole to conceal the fastening of the sleeve to the doublet. They were essential when the detachable sleeves

High necked sleeveless jerkin with wing on the shoulders. Short hip length skirt. The doublet sleeves were tabbed. The ruff at the neck open and hand-ruffs were worn on the cuffs (c.1568).

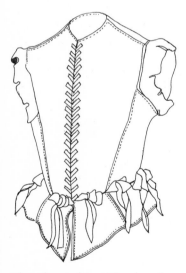

Sleeveless jerkin with a broad skirt, the wings hiding the welts on the shoulders. The centre fastening from neck to waist was by lacing and there were a series of points at the waist.

were in place, to hide the points and ties. Some were narrow and plain, drooping down over the shoulder (1545–1550). Others were wide and flat, shaped over the shoulder and narrowing to the armpit with various edges scalloped or tabbed (1550–1570), or a bunch of looped tabs, often double (1565–1590). Rolls were also placed over the armholes and served the same purpose though they were not considered as wings.

Sleeves followed on from the previous decade with variations. There were padded sleeves which fitted close to the wrist, at which they had a short vertical slit closed with 8–12 buttons (1545–1650). The wide puffed *trunk sleeve* which was also narrow to the wrist and buttoned, was slashed or pinked.

Some sleeves were full, ending in a closed wrist and were often used as pockets to store personal accessories. These latter two types of sleeve were either padded, distended or stiffened with wire or bone and were called *farthingale sleeves*. The full shoulder narrowing to the wrist with the front seam unsewn which followed the previous fashion by being buttoned or tied at close intervals, was popular from 1580–1600.

A fad of the time was to leave a part of the seam open to expose the white shirt beneath. The detachable sleeve followed all the styles of the sleeves mentioned. Sham sleeves were worn, of the hanging variety, and were in vogue during 1575–1630.

Girdles or girdlesteads (also called waistbands) were often shaped to the contours of the doublet waistline. The girdle was made from both leather and material, the leather plain or embossed when made to support a hanger for swords or daggers. For more fashion-conscious and wealthier people the girdles were made from velvets, silks, and interwoven with precious stones or gold and silver; woven tape was used by the lower classes. Eyelet holes were attached to a reinforced canvas band which was sewn on the inside of the doublet lining at waist level, these corresponded to a similar row of eyelet holes attached to the hose, which when points were threaded through joined hose and doublet. These were known as concealed points and were popular during the 1560–1595 period. Visible points (1595–1630) were threaded through from the outside by eyelet holes at the waistline but after this date they became merely ornamental.

JACKET

The jerkin or jacket was neither padded nor busked but usually lined and worn over the doublet. The jacket followed the form of the doublet regardless of its many variations. A standing collar was fashionable in the 1540–1590 period reaching its maximum height in the 1560s, becoming narrower after 1590 when it became a turned-down flat collar onto the shoulders or just a narrow band.

The jacket was closed down the front from the top of the collar to the waistline by a close row of buttons or by hooks and eyes or more uncommonly by lacing or points. The skirt was either long or short, if short, it followed the form of the doublet, if long, it fell to the top of the thigh covering the trunk hose. Sleeves were often absent, but when worn they could be close-fitting, loose, narrowing to the wrist or puffed at the shoulders. Hanging sleeves were worn throughout the century but the mode during the latter part was to wear one sleeve and leave the other hanging. Sham sleeves were hanging streamers without armholes and were merely used as ornamentation often being thrust into the girdle.

The buff jerkin, a military garment, was converted to civilian fashion and called a leather jerkin (1545–1575). The body of the leather jerkin was cut in narrow panes from the chest to the waist with the collar and yoke either plain or pinked, the shoulders being well padded. The sleeves were short, often having wings only. Fastening was by the usual methods down the front or down the side. The skirt portion was short and usually tabbed in pickadils, often paned.

Still popular was the waistcoat (1485–1625) worn under the doublet; this was a decorative, padded, waist-length garment especially worn for warmth.

The gown which had been in fashion for the last 150 years was now worn mainly by professional people or for ceremonial purposes by the nobility. It had changed very little from the previous period, with full folds falling from a fitted yoke. From 1450–1570 it was worn open to knee length and between 1450–1600 it fell to the ankle; it could on occasion be closed by a girdle or sash. From a narrow rever it came over the shoulders into a deep collar which lay over the shoulders, or a standing collar with a very narrow rever edge. The sleeves were the hanging type with slits for the arm to come through. Shoulder puff sleeves had the sham hanging sleeves attached. The trimmings were fur or velvet and linings were silk, satin and taffeta.

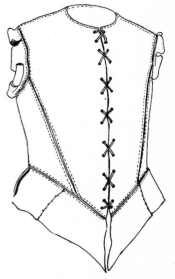

Collarless and sleeveless buff jerkin secured down the front by lacing (1570–1590).

Deep skirted doublet with a small standing collar, the chemise frill visible above. The sleeves were slashed with the chemise cuffs visible at the wrists. The fur-bordered gown reached to mid-calf and had attached hanging sleeves. A Court flat cap with feathers was worn (c.1535).

CAPES AND CLOAKS

The wearing of cloaks was established by the fashionable male from 1545–1600. The wearing of a different cloak for morning, afternoon and evening was a vogue among the wealthier gentlemen of fashion. The general shape and cut was from either a full or three-quarter circle, often slit at the back or sides for the convenience of horse riding. The length varied throughout the period from waist-length, which remained popular throughout, to middle thigh-length and long to the ankles in the latter part of the century.

The neckline also varied, with narrow turned-down collars

which joined a narrow lapel down the front becoming wider down to the hem, or standing collars which could be a full collar or a back part only; in both cases the collar was joined to the lapel which continued down to the hem. A style without either collar or lapel with the edge bordered by a band of trimming was not uncommon. Styles of cloaks and the manner of wear varied with the fashionable trends of the period.

The sleeved cloak, usually short to the thigh and closed with tasselled cords popular after the mid-century, had either puffed or plain shoulder sleeves with hanging sleeves attached.

The short *Spanish cape*, popular for almost a century, had a hood attached at the back – a left-over attachment from the earlier travelling cloak. The hood was wide and pointed and decorated with loops and buttons but was at this time purely ornamental.

The cape was short to the hips later becoming waist length by mid-century, and had a narrow turned-down collar with a narrow lapel from neck to hem. The Spanish cape could be worn either over one or both shoulders. The long French cloak, *manteau a la reitre*, fell to or below the knees, cut in a full or half-circle style. It was fitted with a wide shoulder collar which reached down to the elbows and was usually slung or draped over the left shoulder. The *Dutch cloak* was waist length, wide and fitted with very wide sleeves. The tippet continued to be worn as an extra short shoulder cape with or without a cloak, often being worn with just the gown.

Capes and cloaks came in many types of materials: silk, taffeta, velvet and were decorated with lace, braid, loops and buttons. In accordance with the taste of wearer the colours of cloaks were diverse, many brilliant.

Military wear adapted to civilian purpose became very popular, in particular the *mandilion*, a loose jacket-type garment hanging to the hips and slit at the side forming a back and front panel, which fastened from the neck to the chest and pulled on over the head like the earlier garments of the twelfth and thirteenth century. The collar was short and standing. The sleeves were the hanging type and later became merely sham hanging sleeves. The mandilion was worn either over the shoulders with the sleeves just hanging at the sides or it was worn sideways with the panels covering the shoulders whilst the sleeves hung down the front and the back.

Military type mandilion which could be worn sideways, one sleeve hanging over the front. (1585–1590).

Doublet under short embroidered cape and small closed neck ruff. The upper hose were visible. Hair was closely curled and a small moustache was worn (1578–1580).

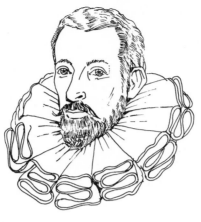

Large cartwheel ruff (c.1587).

Late ruff in flattened figure-of-eight design (c.1598).

Ruff and falling band worn together (c.1597).

Worn mainly by the middle classes was the *cassock*, a wide, hip-length jacket with sleeves either close fitting to the wrist or short to elbow length and fitted with a narrow standing collar. A long wide coat worn with or without a belt and having long wide sleeves was called a *gabardine* and was mainly worn by horsemen.

NECKWEAR

Neckwear during this period either followed the mode of the turned-down collar (falling band) or the pleated or goffered collar, the *ruff*.

The linen turn-down collar varied in shape over the years, coming from the neckband of the shirt and turned down to cover the collar of the doublet; small at first, increasing in width later in the century, it gradually spread and lay flat over the shoulders. At the latter end of the century it was no longer closed at the throat and became a separate item. Also in this period heavy laced borders were worn.

The goffered ruff which originated from the frilled neck-band of the chemise became fashionable in the 1560s. The frill became larger in size and, with the invention of starch, the ruff soon became a separate article. Ruffs were attached under the chin by means of cords or tasselled strings.

Like most fashions the ruff had its variations; for example the small ruff, which was, in the earlier part of the period, attached to the shirt, and then later as a separate item was in most cases worn open at the throat in front, and, in the 1560–1570 period, a small closed ruff. From the 1570s a medium-size ruff was popular, this being closed all round. After 1580 the size of ruffs increased to immense proportions and became known as *cartwheel ruffs* and were closed all round. Common to all ruffs, the band strings which attached them were tied and concealed.

The construction and fabrication of the ruff became a very complicated business as well as, for certain merchants, a very profitable one. From a very simple single pleated frill they became, in the latter part of the century, arranged into three or more layers. Setting-pokers were used to make tubular sets or pleats. These pokers were heated and placed onto the starched linen and thus formed the sets.

Although coloured starch was used, its popularity seemed to be confined to the few as most contemporary portraits show either white or a creamy yellow/off-white. Supports for ruffs came from, first, the pikadils which were used, as they had been earlier, as a tabbed decoration for the standing-collar, then fitted with a stiffened frame and turned out horizontally to support the ruff. For the larger, later medium, and cartwheel types came the *underpropper* or *supportasse*, which, as their names imply, were wire frames to prop up or support the massive neckwear decorations. These frames spread out from the doublet collar to which they was attached, and were so arranged that they gave a tilt at the back and a downward slope in the front; the starched ruff was placed over them.

Wrist-wear generally followed the fashion of collars. Worn with the falling band was a turned back cuff edged in lace although this was sometimes worn with a ruff too. A small ruff-type frill was worn at the wrist matching the ruff at the neck.

LEG-WEAR

There were at this period two variations of leg-wear. The first were the *long hose*, a combination of long stockings and breeches joined together to make a single article of clothing. This type of leg-wear continued in use for about 200 years (*c*.1400–1620). During the 1570s breeches and stockings were worn as separate items. The variations in leg-wear were many. For example, the long stockinged hose had, in the early part of the period, oval-shaped extensions from the crotch outwards. *The trunk hose*, worn from the mid-century

*Short collarless Spanish cloak.
The doublet has a slightly
protruding peascod belly with a
narrow skirt. Trunk hose with
canions are worn and the
stockings pulled up over them.
On the feet are pantoffles or
mules. A bonnet with ostrich and
osprey feathers and decoration
round the edge is seen carried in
the hand (c.1575).*

onwards, had many names: *French hose, slops, trunk breeches*
and *round hose*. At first they resembled an onion shape coming
out from the waist to mid-thigh, often called *Spanish kettle-
drums* after the Spanish fashion they followed. From the
1570s they sloped out from the waist to mid-thigh then
turned inwards, and became very close-fitting amongst the
ultra fashionable. This style became incorporated with
canions which were tube-like extensions from the trunk hose
and fitted over the thigh and fell to the knee or just below.
They were usually of a different colour and material and were
always fully lined. They could be fastened either over or
under the separate stockings.

The *pluder-hose* was a German or Swiss adoption from

hose worn by mercenary soldiers and although seen in England was not too popular. A type of trunk hose, they were similar in style to the breeches of the period, but consisted of two pairs, one worn inside the other. The outer pair was made up of four to six broad panes of 15cm width, the gaps filled in by materials of different colours, the bagginess overhanging the panes below. The inner pair were made of a finer material but much longer and wider. To obtain such a full effect, four to six metres of material were required, the stuffing had a further requirement of some 40 to 60 metres.

The crotch appendage, the cod-piece, was still worn with the trunk hose, but gradually became smaller from about 1540. From 1590 it was unfashionable, and finally discarded altogether by the end of the century. The stuffing of the cod-piece was achieved by hair or canvas with a lining of silk or taffeta. The cod-piece was used sometimes as a pocket or pouch, often embroidered and tied with points or coloured ribbons.

BREECHES

Breeches, which were worn with separate stockings, were a Spanish fashion popularized by Venetians and evolved in England into three variants. In the 1570s to 1580s they were very close fitting, the stockings being either pulled up and gartered above the knee, or closed over the stocking below the knee. Also fashionable at this time were *Venetian breeches*, full and wide at the top and gathered in at the waist, padded round the hips then narrowed to the knees, where just below the knee they were fastened with silk points, the edges ending in a row of lace. Others were baggy and voluminous without pleats which, early in the seventeenth century, became pleated and gathered from the waist to the knee, these were called *Venetian slops* or *Wide Venetians*.

The Dutch fashion of *open breeches* became more popular in the seventeenth century. They were not unlike modern shorts and often had openings up the sides to reveal the fancy garters fastened above the knee, or if the slits were not present, showing only the fringe of the garters. Pockets were often inserted in the lining of the breeches.

The pouch or cod-piece disappeared from all types of breeches and was replaced by a vertical slit in front which was concealed by the folds of the material. 'Trussing the points', continued to be the method of fastening the hose to the doublet.

*Upper class mother and son
walking in the country with a
male attendant (c.1574).*

UNDERWEAR

Long white linen drawers were worn under breeches and were cut full, being knee length and tied in front with ribbons, and taped behind over a short opening. When worn long, they could have feet attached or bands holding them down, passing beneath the instep.

Shoe, close fitting to the ankle and tied with a bow.

STOCKINGS

Stockings which met the breeches at the knee still continued to be called *netherstocks*, they were tailored from yarn, silk or wool and cut on the cross and clocked in various patterns at the ankles in coloured thread. The tailored stockings were soon to be replaced by the knitted stockings which were made by hand until 1589 when the stocking frame came into use. Stockings knitted in silk were very expensive. For warmth two or even three pairs of stockings could be worn, indeed short socks were not unknown and were often worn for the extra warmth.

With the advent of silk stockings, *boot-hose* developed. They originated as unfashionable but practical stockings, worn to protect the silk stockings from wear on the boots. Later they became more ornamental, being embroidered and lace-edged and made of more delicate material. The tops, which were bound or stitched were attached to the breeches with decorative points (laces with metal ends). These were, in fact, the forerunner of the present-day suspenders and garters.

Garters were indeed very fashionable and were not used just to hold the stocking in place but as showy accessories. They were worn just below the knee and fastened in a bow on the outside of the leg, or above the knee when wearing the closer fitting Venetians or canions when the stocking was pulled up over the breeches. Often worn with the latter style was cross-gartering, which came in about 1560 and lasted to the end of the century – the style which was ridiculed by Shakespeare in Malvolio in *Twelfth Night* (1600). The garter was attached to just below the knee in front; the ends were taken back, then twisted across behind the knee and then pulled forward to above the knee, where the ends were fastened into a bow, which could be placed either in front or on the outside of the leg.

Cross gartering around the knee (c.1595).

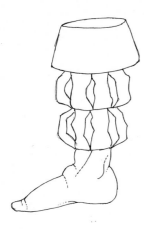

Square-toed, low-heeled shoe heel and decorated with a rosette

Tall boot, slashed and cuffed, tied with a tab and bow.

Slashed high boot with cuff.

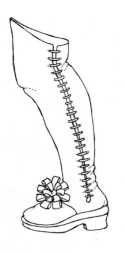

Over the knee riding boot with heel. At the front a rosette was worn as decoration. The boot was laced at the side.

SHOES AND BOOTS

A kind of legging popular from about 1509 and known as *startups* was a high-fitting shoe worn mainly in the country by the lower classes.

Boots and buskins, worn only for riding or by the military, reached just above knee level and were loose fitting. They were often slit at the top of the back seam to facilitate movement. The tops, as previously, were still turned back to reveal the lining of contrasting colour.

Some leather boots were very decorative and tight fitting, shaped to the legs and laced by points to the breeches at the sides. Slashings at the knee revealed silks and taffetas in different colours.

Buskins, lined with fur were made of a softer leather or could even be made of velvet.

Pattens, although still worn in their original styles (see Vol. I), evolved into overshoes with wooden soles which could either have just a toepiece into which shoes fitted or, alternatively, an open leather vamp with thongs for fastening. Aspen, being a light wood, was used and the sole was often carved leaving just cross bars under the heel and instep. Pattens could occasionally also be made of leather.

To protect the hunters, fishermen and country people from mud, long leather leggings or high-laced boots made of untanned leather called *cockers* became popular around 1514.

Plain buckled straps were also in use, and were closed just below the knee, the stockings were folded back completely concealing both buckle and strap.

It was very fashionable to wear all types of head-wear in the house, on all formal occasions, and always whilst eating. Dancing also encouraged certain types of head-wear. The flat fashion remained until the late 1560s then gradually began to gain height until by the end of the century very high-crowned hats were the fashion.

The flat cap remained in fashion until the 1570s and continued to be worn until the end of the century and even later by business men, the cap then being called the *city flat cap*. The *statute cap* – a knitted close cap – was ordered to be worn by an Act of Parliament of 1571; the order stated that all people above the age of six years, except those of high rank by birth or degree, should wear a cap of wool on the sabbath and all holy days and one which had been manufactured in England. As this order was continually disobeyed it was repealed in 1597.

From the 1560s until the end of the century the narrow-brimmed raised soft-crown bonnet was in fashion. The crown varied in height according to the wearer, sometimes it was extended to its full height ceasing to be flat at the top; sometimes it was worn at a rakish angle and often just perched on the head. For ornamentation a feather could be attached. From the 1580s the soft crown was stiffened with buckram folded and pleated into the narrow brim and always worn at an angle.

The tall brimless *Monmouth cap* came to be worn in the 1580s by the military and the navy ratings of the period.

From the early 1560s the fashion of wearing a high conical crowned *copotain* became very fashionable. This tall felt hat had a fairly moderate brim which was dressed in various ways: flat, turned up, turned down, or rolled round the edge like a modern bowler hat brim. This was also worn at a tilt and after the late 1580s was invariably worn with a backward tilt. Throughout the century this type of hat manifested a variety of styles, the crowns being high or low, brims alternating from narrow to moderate or wide, textures stiff and soft. Materials for hats varied from felt, beaver, leather to wool or woven silk. Linings were of silks, satins and taffeta. Bonnets were made from knitted wool, felt, and fur, and lined in the same way as hats. Straw hats were worn by lower class country people.

Hat and bonnet accessories included highly decorated hat bands made from silken cords or metallic materials such as

Bonnet with a full pleated crown on a small brim. A small open ruff was worn at the neck (c.1563).

Tall, soft bonnet with feathers on one side and an embroidered band round the narrow brim (c.1575).

TOP: *Close-fitting low décolletage bodice with slashed shoulder wings (c.1585).*
LEFT: *Boy in long hose and falling collar (c.1590).*
RIGHT: *Trunk hose with canions, slight peascod body doublet with ruff (c.1590).*

LEFT: *Wealthy merchant in a copotain hat, cloak, cassock and breeches with decorative garters (c.1598).*
CENTRE: *Countrywoman with large straw hat and large white apron (c.1605).*
RIGHT: *Country worker wearing thigh length belted mediaeval type tunic (c.1563).*

Boy wearing a bonnet with the full crown pleated on to a narrow brim. Decoration was by means of a drooping ostrich feather on one side (c.1558).

Lace neck ruff supported by pickadils which were attached to a high standing collar buttoned in front (c.1577).

High crowned hat trimmed with a jewelled hat band and ostrich feather. The neck ruff was embroidered (c.1578).

Boy wearing an extended soft-crowned cap pleated on to a narrow brim. He is also wearing a lace ruff (c.1580).

Soft velvet hat with a narrow brim, and a coif worn beneath

High crowned hat with a large band. A jewelled hat brooch and ostrich and osprey feather tips completed the decoration. A large cartwheel-type ruff was also worn (c.1586).

gold, silver and copper. Semi-precious stones were very popular as were buttons plain and crystal. Pearls and diamonds were worn by the very rich who also favoured feathers of ostrich topped with osprey usually on the right-hand side.

Undercaps usually made of white linen were still worn under the hats and bonnets and by court officials such as lawyers, these being fastened under the chin. *Skull caps* and black coifs were worn only by the elderly.

From the 1570s the wearing of nightcaps became very

fashionable and continued until the eighteenth century. This type of headwear was worn by all classes, the difference being only in the workmanship and the materials used. The basic shape was a deep round crown with a turned-up brim set in close to the crown and made in one piece. For those who could afford it the hat was highly embroidered and made from linen, velvet, brocades and silks. For the poorer people they were often made of an inferior material without decoration and with the addition of ear flaps as they could on occasions be worn out-of-doors.

HAIR-STYLES AND BEARDS

From the 1560s hair became very close cropped and brushed upwards into a bristle effect often accomplished with the aid of gum. Later in the Elizabethan era, men were extremely conscious of their coiffure which, from 1580 became very elaborate, with tight curls crimped all over the head. During the 1590s hair became longer, falling to shoulder length, the front fringe pulled back from the face and arranged to one side with, sometimes, a small lock of hair allowed to dangle down in front.

Black coif, usually worn by older men (c.1564).

During the same period the *love-lock* became fashionable; this was a length of hair grown long at the neck, curled and brought forward to hang over the shoulder and down onto the chest. Often a single rose was worn in the hair under the cap.

Until the middle of the sixteenth century, beards of all kinds were worn. Their names were in most cases perfect descriptions of their styles: *forked, spade, whispy, vandyke* and, less easily understandable, the *pickdevant* which was a short brushed up moustache and beard combined. The wearing of both beards and moustaches was very fashionable.

During Queen Elizabeth's reign beards could be starched and powdered, perfumed and waved and occasionally dyed fashionable saffron red. They were styled with curling irons and shaped in various ways. They could be pointed, square or round as well as 'T' shaped or oblong.

ACCESSORIES

Gloves were worn either short or with gauntlets either plain or with embroidery and fringes. Popular were scented gloves imported from Spain. Later in the century gloves were manufactured in England and became commonplace. Materials varied from silks, satins, velvets to worsted

Hair worn with a centre parting, as well as a forked beard and small moustache (c.1580).

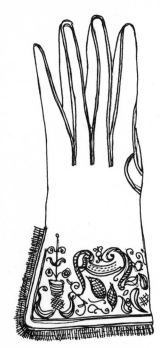

Glove with embroidered cuff (c.1603).

Detachable neck ruff worn with a high-necked military gorget (c.1577).

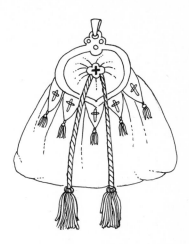

Leather bag with cords and tassels (c.1575).

Mitten with one large bag for the fingers and a smaller one for the thumb. The palm could have a horizontal slit to allow the fingers to protrude (c.1590).

materials, wool and skins.

Handkerchiefs remained very decorative and were carried in the hand, but with the advent of pockets and the deep folds in the doublets, handkerchiefs were now often stuffed out of sight. As an elegant accessory they were, nevertheless, very fashionable with edgings of lace and embroidery often being trimmed with elegant cutwork designs, buttons and fringed tassels. Materials were linen, lawn, and imported velvet.

Scarves were introduced in the 1580s but were not fashionable wear, being worn principally for warmth. The wearing of a scarf draped from one shoulder was taken up by the more fashion-conscious nobility.

The *girdle* had stayed in fashion throughout the century. It was narrow and curved to the waist, closed in the front with a clasp or buckle.

The drawn string type *purse*, made in leather, silk or some worsted material, was still carried either attached to the girdle or enclosed in the folds of the doublet or in the pockets. Fashions were often taken from the military by ultra-fashion-conscious young men, among which was the wearing of the *gorget*. The gorget was a symbolic piece of armour in the form of a steel collar worn in the 1560s and early into the next century.

Swords and *daggers* were usually confined to the military and nobility. The slender rapier replaced the heavier sword for the nobility and was worn also with a dagger on the right hip in a horizontal position from a chain attached to the girdle.

Long wooden walking sticks with a knob of metal were carried, but they were not accepted by the fashionable at this period, their use being almost totally confined to the elderly. The more fashionable fops of the day carried fans and mirrors either on their person or in their hats.

Occasionally *masks* were worn by men, their use confined to that of hiding their identity. Similar to the women's fashion they were made from silk, velvet or satin and lined with various other materials including skins. Often they were held in place by a button on the inside and gripped by the teeth.

Necks, ears, fingers and clothing were heavily festooned with jewellery both in precious and semi-precious stones. Rings with both real and sham stones adorned the fingers.

Women

Many male fashions were worn by women during this century; for example the doublet, often worn in place of the kirtle bodice, also the waistcoat, mainly worn for warmth, as were the coat, the cassock and the gabardine.

The cuffs of many garments were finished in small hand ruffs or laced turned-back cuffs, made from lawn, cambric and materials used for making the neck wear. The cloak was still worn, it was usually large and now more for travelling than a fashionable item.

Although many of the previous fashions continued to be worn, a woman's dress, began to be made as two separate articles of clothing: the bodice and the kirtle, now more often called the petticoat. The bodice, often strangely called 'a pair of Bodies' by the Elizabethans, was a stiff corset-like garment, supported with stays made from whalebone, metal or wood and often referred to as 'busks', although the term busk was the name given to the tie or point which fastened the stay into its sheath. The kirtle followed the shape of the farthingale, either the French or the Spanish.

BODICE

During the period 1545–1590 the bodice was close-fitting and ended with a short point at the waistline and was closed on the left-hand side by hooks and eyes. Both high and low necklines were in fashion. When the neckline was low (from

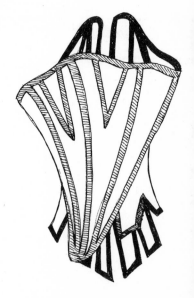

Linen basquine or fitted and boned hip length type of corset with whalebone stiffeners (c.1580).

Close-fitting bodice with large shoulder wings. Slashed bishop-type sleeves were joined by points and bows. Large open hanging sleeves tied with bows, attached at the shoulders dropped almost to ground level (c.1596).

Close-fitting bodice with pickadils or tabs and a small circular neck ruff the neck and shoulders covered with embroidery. Large slashed wings were encrusted with jewels (c.1583).

about mid-century to the 1580s) it was usually square with a gentle curve over the bosom. The décolletage could be concealed by a high-necked chemise, which was decorated with a standing collar and short frill that had a short V-shape opening at the throat. After 1560 the chemise was often discarded and the ruff worn by itself with the décolletage exposed. Sometimes a partlet 'fill-in' was worn which had a standing collar open at the throat to reveal the chemise frilled collar.

Often the partlet, decorated with semi-precious stones, was of material in a contrasting colour to the bodice, but matching the sleeves or forepart. The high-necked fashion was the usual standing collar attached to the bodice, the collar being open at the throat or with the narrow Medici collar. The open neck of the chemise always exposed the frill shown above the collar.

From the 1560s the high standing collar was topped by a separate ruff. The large closed cartwheel ruff became fashion-

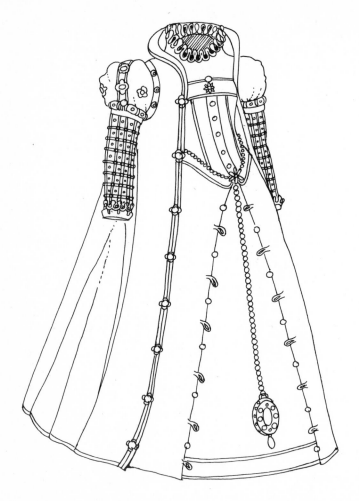

Long trained velvet coat had short puffed sleeves. The overbodice had a square neckline revealing the underbodice with the close-fitting sleeves and a high collar. The bodice was pointed at the waist. Ruffs were worn around the neck and wrists (c.1569).

able in the 1570s and took the place of the smaller ruff. With the high collar the bodice was closed down the centre front either with buttons or with hooks and eyes.

Until the 1560s funnel-shaped sleeves remained in vogue. Tight fitting to the elbow they then developed suddenly to a large opening and ended with a wide turned-back cuff in front and a hanging streamer fashion at the back. The undersleeve was full and closed at the wrist and emerged from the large cuff in a slashed design with the frilled cuff of the chemise visible at the wrist.

From *c*.1560 the long close-fitting sleeve which was slightly bombasted was decorated with slashes and puffs of the chemise, the wrist ended in a hand ruff.

Sleeves had their variations: slashed and puffed, small round shoulder, double and single slashed roll wings and spreading welts round the armholes. Hanging sleeves were worn and after *c.*1560 became sham. The close-fitting sleeve had a number of bands gathered in the length of the arm and was hence called the *gathered sleeve*. Popular was a full puffed-out sleeve which finished with a deep cuff at elbow length under which was a detachable close fitting to the wrist sleeve often of a different material from the puffed shoulder piece. Full, falling from the shoulder to the wrist, with a close-fitting cuff ending in a small hand ruff, was the *bishop sleeve*.

After about 1580 the bodice remained close-fitting but the point at the waistline now became much longer. The low neckline fashion was worn with a stomacher front. To accommodate this, the bodice was cut with a deep V-shape opening to a deep point at the front and was supported by being fitted around the neck at the back. The edges, usually guarded or embroidered, could start narrow then increase at the shoulders to form a flat turned-down collar, across the shoulders and down the back.

The *stomacher* was fastened to the bodice by ties which were usually attached on the inside edge making them invisible. Sometimes the décolletage was filled in by the high-standing chemise collar which was gathered in front, in place of the stomacher. The neck was surmounted by a ruff at all times, often large like the popular cartwheel ruff. The wired collar, *rebato*, or the *fan-shaped ruff*, were worn mainly by single women.

Towards the latter part of the century (1575–1585) sleeves became large and bombasted, the full bishop sleeves became wider with padding. The *demi-cannon* sleeve was stiffly padded with buckram and wire or whalebone, pinked and slashed, puckered and trimmed with lace. Turned-back lace cuffs were usual but were also worn together with a small hand ruff.

SKIRTS AND FARTHINGALES

The skirt cut either in the French or Spanish farthingale style was often draped up at the sides to reveal the richly embroidered underskirt when the farthingale was not being worn. The farthingale only very slowly became fashionable but eventually became very popular and was worn by all classes. The *Spanish farthingale* (1545–1590) was the first style to reach England, the *French farthingale* followed (1580–1620).

The farthingale was an imaginative undergarment which made the hips appear as wide as the length of the body and stood out at right angles. It was made of a variety of paddings, whalebones, wire, wood and wickerwork, and fastened around the waist, balancing above it by means of a *basquine*, a kind of corset, thus making the entire silhouette a very unnatural shape.

The basquine was a fitted, boned, hip-length garment, laced up. It was made of a stiff material, fitting tight at the waist, widening, funnel shaped, hiding the bosom beneath a false front over which the dress was worn.

The formation of the Spanish farthingale, also known as a *verdingale*, was a series of circular hoops made of 'bents' or hoops, of wire, whalebone or wood which became wider in circumference from the waist downwards until they made a large circle round the feet, thus producing the characteristic funnel shape. However, like all fashion the shape did vary from a funnel shape to a bell or dome shape and often only one hoop at the hem of the farthingale was worn. The skirt was either gored to produce the flat stiff effect from the waist to the hem, smooth and without pleats or evenly pleated all round to produce the effect known as 'a round kirtle'. The wearing of a trained farthingale was uncommon for classes other than the nobility who wore them only on ceremonial and court occasions.

Popular was the inverted V-shape at the front which revealed the plain underskirt of the kirtle or farthingale, this was covered by a 'forepart' – a highly decorative embroidered under-petticoat.

The French farthingale was Queen Elizabeth's favourite, and was worn at Court as early as the 1560s. The two main styles were the roll and the wheel variety, both basically cylindrical from the waist to the ground.

The roll farthingale known as the *bum roll*, was a bombasted padded roll worn round the hips. It was not unlike a swimmer's life-belt with a small opening in the front to which ties were attached. It was worn to give an upward tilt at the back, similar to the *demi-circle farthingale* also worn at this period and which, as its name implies, was merely half a roll at the back, both giving a sloping-to-the-front effect.

The later *wheel farthingale* (1580–1620) had other names – *Catherine wheel* and *Italian farthingale*. A wheel-shaped construction of stiffeners of wire and whalebone were formed round the waist, the width at right angles to the waist measured 130cm or less according to the dictates of fashion, but was always worn with the tilt-up at the back. The whole was usually covered by a damask material or silk. The skirt

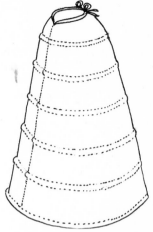

Spanish farthingale tied at the waist with a ribbon (c.1550).

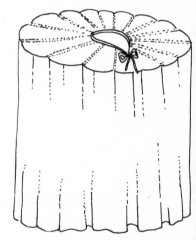

French farthingale, cylindrical in shape (c.1580).

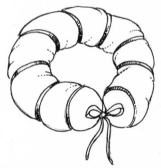

Roll farthingale or bum roll worn around the hips (c.1575).

High-necked loose gown with a small ruff at the neck fastened by ribbons down the front. Both fitchets and edges were fur-lined. The short puffed shoulder sleeves revealed the close fitting ornamented undersleeves with wrist ruffs (c.1559).

was made very full so that it would fit over the hoop, gathered in, then allowed to fall to ground level to give the cylindrical effect. A narrow inverted V-shape opening ran down the front, often barely revealing ᴜᴇ forepart which lay beneath. Towards the end of the century the tilt became a little more exaggerated and extra padding in the form of *cushionets* were inserted under the structures to increase the angle of the slope.

To cover the stark outline of the hoops a flounced skirt was worn. This was a circular piece of material ruched up to form a large ruff effect round the waist, forming horizontal folds or sets which slightly overlapped the edge.

Ladies and gentlemen of fashion: showing a front and back view of the gable headdress with falling lappets (c.1535).

GOWN

The warm overgarment, the gown, was still in fashion from about 1545 to the 1620s. Close-fitting to the shoulders it fell to the ground in heavy folds, spreading out at ground level. The inverted V-shape opening at the front from the neck-line to the hem exposed the dress beneath.

Collar variations included open or closed with ties, high standing collar, or narrow round collar which joined the lapels down the front of the gown and the narrow turn-over collar. These collars were often allowed to remain open, but if fastened they were closed with a button, ties or buttons-and-loops.

The gown followed the fashionable arrangements of sleeves – short to the elbow and puffed out at the shoulder or long hanging sleeves with openings at the elbow and wings at the shoulders. Often no sleeves were present, the armholes being decorated with welts or rolls. Another type of gown fitted the figure closely to the waist then extended over the hips falling in heavy pleats to the ground; this was the *close-bodied* gown worn during the whole of the period and had either a ruff or a high Medici collar. The front fastening was with ribbon points or button-and-loops. At hip level were the placket slits through which articles attached to the girdle could be easily reached, these placket slits or fitchets were usually embroidered round the edges.

NECK-WEAR

In the 1560s neck ruffs evolved from the chemise neck frill, which was joined to the high neckline to the separate ruff, usually open at the front, which stayed in fashion till the 1570s. The giant *cartwheel ruff* came into popularity in the 1580s lasting into the next century, and was worn with both high and low necklines. The *fan ruff* was wired to come from the sides and back of the low décolletage forming a fan shape at the back of the head.

The *rabato* was also a wire frame shaped and fastened to the low décolletage, the wire outline being filled in with several layers of material and edged in lace.

The *rail*, continued in fashion now becoming like a large shawl of a fine flimsy material, very decorative and some-times starched. The later style of head rail in the 1590s was wired and formed into an arch shape over the head and the diaphanous material from which it was made continued from the wire frame to fall down over the shoulders and back.

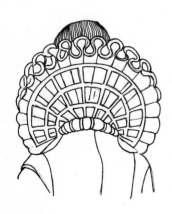

Underpropper, following the male style of wire supports for a large ruff (c.1574).

UNDERWEAR AND STOCKINGS

From the sixteenth century women started to wear *drawers*, a type of trouser tied around the waist and reaching down to the knees and fastened to the stockings with gaiters. Made of cotton or fustian (a material used mainly for underwear) they were originally worn for horse riding. They were later made of silks and brocades and elegant enough to be allowed to be visible beneath the gowns. Stockings were cut on the cross from material and tailored to fit and by about 1600 most hose were fitted as the stocking frame was developed *c.*1589. These stockings were superior as they enhanced the appearance of both legs and shoes, giving the ankle more shape. Above the ankle they could be decorated with clocks which were embroidered. Silk stockings were worn by the upper classes, whilst the lower classes wore mainly woollen.

Socks and garters were worn by both male and female. The garters were an extension of the ornamental ribbon bands, which could be adorned with jewels and fringed gold lace. Cross-gartered ribbons were worn by ladies. As stockings became more popular and fitted, a band of material, buckled and embroidered was worn at the knee.

SHOES

Shoes similar to men's were worn by women, often with pattens; boots, however, were rarely worn.

There were no built-up heels on shoes until about 1600, although wedge heels were experimented with around 1598. To make the soles thicker, cork was used.

HEAD-WEAR

The *attifet*, a type of French hood, had a wired edge to enable the headdress to stand away from the head. It formed an arc either side of the forehead and was covered by a veil which fell in a point over the forehead. In black for widows (although Mary Queen of Scots wore one in white) it has remained in fashion as a widow's peak and cap and also as part of a nun's attire. The attifet originated as a heart-shaped chaperon, the sides being curved over puffs of hair and the front pointed down to the forehead. It was derived from the jewelled coifs and caps of the middle of the sixteenth century.

Coifs were worn indoors and for night attire or as a basis for hoods and hats. They had a seam across the top of the head and the front could be straight or more popularly shaped to a point or curve over the forehead to reveal the hair. A

Girl in a small lace edged hood with a barbe under the chin (c.1558).

Decorated shoe with heel
attached to a low platform.

Ornamented high heeled shoe
mounted on a sole.

Mule with leather sole and heel.

Highly decorative shoe with two
heels.

Leather shoe with diamond
cut-out design.

Mule on a decorated platform.

Chopine with a decorated
leather band across the centre.

Square backed chopine covered
in cork with a slash design on
the attached mule or pantoffle.

Leather shoe popular by men
and women, with a large cut-out
design revealing the coloured
hose.

Country type shoe worn by men
and women, with a single bar
fastening with a buckle.

triangular piece of material matching that of the coif could be worn with the point either to the front or back, and was tied under the chin or the back of the head as desired, and was worn mainly at night. The coif was made of a plain linen, or fustian for nights, but of a decorated or patterned material for day use. The designs were quite elaborate and could be of flowers, birds or animals.

A muffler was worn as protection against the cold by the middle class with a coif or hat.

'Lettice' caps, gable and French hoods remained popular until the 1580s, although the beret types became less popular from about 1560.

Married women wore hats both out and indoors but the younger single girls wore none and allowed their hair to be seen.

From Elizabeth's reign until about 1595, the *taffeta pipkin*, worn over a caul or net, was in favour. It was made of stiffened taffeta with a pleated crown and narrow brim which was either straight or curved. For adornment jewels and buttons as well as long drooping or short tufts of feathers were used. The *court bonnet* was also worn at this period. This consisted of a small velvet cap without a brim, trimmed as was the taffeta pipkin. The feathers were usually white, although a mixture of white and red or just red were also worn. As hats gained in popularity more shapes were adopted. They were made in a variety of materials such as silk, velvet, taffeta, leather, felt and beaver.

The middle class and country women preferred a kind of bowler hat, flat topped and squarish with a narrow or broad brim. Large plain plaited straw hats were worn by country women when working in the open in summer. The art of making straw hats originated in Tuscany.

The fashionable ladies favoured the more exaggerated styles of high-crowned hats, probably due to their hair styles being so elaborate. Their hats were worn mainly for riding and travelling. Although dark colours were usual, the hats could be in any colour. Those made of finer materials were often quilted or richly embroidered with coloured or gold and silver thread.

Hatbands which were a significant part of the hats could be in any colour or material and were often plaited or twisted. If they were left as flat bands, they were encrusted with jewels, gold or enamelled buttons and richly embroidered.

Taffeta pipkin with feather decoration, worn over a hair net (1557–1580).

Amongst older women the French hood remained in fashion with slight variations from about 1550. The hair which had been worn in rolls either side of a centre parting, was now completely hidden by the hood with the hanging piece at the back becoming narrower.

In the 1580s a combined hood and cloak made of a thick material was worn. It was wired to form an arched covering over the head and extending over the face, sometimes curving downwards in the centre. The length of the cloak varied from full length to only waist length and was attached to the shoulder or waist allowing the material to drape down from the back of the head.

During the later years of Elizabeth's reign, 1558–1603, younger married women wore their hair uncovered for the first time. Jewelled ornamentations or small net cauls were still worn however.

In the sixteenth century amongst the refugees were many French and Dutch hatters. These popularized the felt hats worn by men from the 1570s.

HAIR-STYLES

The fashionable hair-style of the 1540s was a centre parting with the hair either rolled or waved back at the temples over padded rolls. Also popular was frizzed or closely curled hair with a reticulated and jewelled cap or caul lined in coloured silks which enclosed the back hair which was plaited or coiled in a bun at the nape of the neck. The cauls were also sometimes made of gold or silver mesh.

A simple hair style, popular first in Venice, became more ornate in the 1560s and 1570s. It had a centre parting with the sides of the hair placed over crescent-shaped pads either side of the head which met in the centre. The hair at the back could be coiled at the nape of the neck and occasionally small curls were seen in front of the ears.

Hair was often fluffed at the sides with a centre parting but by about 1570 it was turned on to pads and raised on wire supports known as *palisadoes*. To make the hair seem thicker a great deal of false hair was used.

Wigs were first introduced into England *c.*1572 and became very fashionable, Queen Elizabeth owning a great number of them. Hair *bodkins* were much worn by most classes. These were jewelled pendants or brooches attached to wires or pins and fastened to either the hair supports or wigs. Feathers also became a popular form of ornamentation, as

Heart-shaped wire, heavily jewelled structure built around the head. Large lace ruff also worn with this head attire (c.1589).

were *head-ties* similar to the billiments of the French hood. They formed a border on the crown of the hair. They could be attached to a cap or caul or were on a band, or could even be the back portion of the French hood.

Combs were made mainly of ivory or boxwood, and a cloth was worn to protect clothes when the hair was combed.

Larger pads or wired frames were used in the 1570s and 1580s and the hair was pulled back over these without a parting.
Such pads gave a higher and wider appearance and were slightly dipped in the front to give a heart-shaped effect. Where necessary the hair was plucked at the temples to attain this effect, or small flat curls were arranged in this manner.

The most popular hair colour of the period was either fair or red, and dyeing was extremely popular. False hair such as dyed horse hair was added to give the appearance of thickness.

Head-rails were much favoured by Queen Elizabeth. These veils were encrusted with jewels and made of a transparent material, wired to curve behind the head and fasten to the shoulders. In the 1590s the heart-shaped effect became less popular and by about 1600 the hair began to be brushed high, curls and frizzing going out of fashion.

ACCESSORIES

Sweet gloves or perfumed gloves were very popular and worn by both male and female, these were called 'Frangipani gloves'. Made from velvet, silk and satin for domestic wear, leather and doeskin were worn for horse riding. Embroidered mittens were also popular towards the end of the century.

Aprons were worn by the lower classes as a domestic accessory and by the wealthier as a fashionable accessory. They were made for working people in flannel, canvas and heavier materials and for richer people in linen, silks and taffetas, usually trimmed in lace.

Embroidered lace-edged handkerchiefs similar to those carried by men were edged with fringes and tassels and made in lawn, linen and silk.

Mufflers started to become fashionable towards the 1550s for the upper classes and became a popular fashion for the middle classes during Queen Elizabeth's reign (1558–1603). The muffler was a type of headscarf worn around the lower part of the face and fastened at the back. For the wealthy it was made of velvet and sable and was worn in winter as protection against the cold.

Girdles were still worn to carry various articles of a personal nature as in earlier periods. String-drawn purses of leather, velvet, satin or other rich materials were supported by ribbons or chains to the girdle. Fans, both large and small, usually made of feathers with an elabroate handle, often with a small mirror inlaid, were also attached to the girdle. Small muffs from skins of animals were also attached to the girdle belt by ribbons.

Either covering the whole or half of the face was the fashion of mask wearing from the 1550s onwards. Masks were worn for the protection of the complexion (sun-tanned skin being extremely unfashionable) and to avoid being recognized. They came in various shapes but were usually oval with holes for the eyes and were made from skins, silks and satins; sometimes a button was attached on the inside so that it could be held in place by the teeth.

Glossary

Aiglets	Metal points or tabs attached to the ends of ribbons, laces or ties.
Attifet	Headdress forming an arc above forehead and covered with a veil falling to a heart shape in front.
Barbe	Long piece of linen, pleated and worn under the chin.
Billiments	Decorated border for French hoods. Set in gold were precious stones on a foundation matching the hood. These designs often corresponded to the borders and girdles of the gowns, as well as the necklaces.
Bodkin	Long, pointed ornamental pin.
Bombast	Padding of horsehair, wool, flax or cotton etc.
Bongrace	Flat, stiff projection, shading the face from the sun. If worn alone or over a coif it projected in front and hung down loosely behind. If worn as part of the French hood, the hanging part behind was turned up over the crown and extended over the forehead.
Buff Jerkin	Military type jacket made of hide, worn over a doublet, occasionally without sleeves, but with wings only.
Bum Roll	Also known as Roll Farthingale.
Buskins	High boots reaching to the knees in leather when worn for riding, or of velvet or satin or a softer leather for ladies.
Canions	Extensions from the trunk hose fitting to the thigh down to the knees and lined in a contrasting colour. Stockings were pulled over these.
Cartwheel Ruff	Starched circular wide collar, cartwheel shaped and tied under the chin, with the front edges apart in an inverted V shape.
Cassock	Long, loose overcoat, buttoned from neck to hem.
Caul	Close fitting, reticulated skull cap becoming more bag shaped at the back to hold the hair in the 1540s.
Chaperon	Short, caped hood.
Chemise	Under-garment made of fine linen.
Chopines	High, wooden stilts worn as overshoes with the toecap fixed to a wood or cork sole.
Cockers	Knee-high laced boots or leggings, made of untanned leather.
Cod-piece	Decorated pouch concealing the front opening of men's breeches padded and often used for containing money and handkerchiefs.
Coif	Close-fitting cap, sometimes worn as an undercap, but if worn alone embroidered. It curved forward over the ears and could be fastened under the chin.
Copotain	Hat with high crown in a cone shape with a small, occasionally rolled-up brim.

Cornet	Horned cap, similar to the bongrace, usually worn with a French hood.
Court Bonnet	Small bonnet with the crown gathered to a band or rolled brim and decorated with small feathers and jewels.
Décolletage	Low neckline of bodice.
Demi-gown	Short gown, often worn when riding. Fashionable 1500–1560.
Doublet	Padded jacket, close fitting and waisted.
Dutch Cloak	Short, decorated cloak with wide sleeves.
English Hood	Hood with pointed arch over forehead. Front hair hidden by striped silk tubes crossing over under the arch. The back of the hood was diamond shaped, from which hung lappets.
Falling Band Collar	Lace-edged, turned down collar, also later known as a Vandyke collar.
Fitchet	Placket hole made vertically in the skirt.
Frangipani Gloves	Also known as Sweet Gloves. They were scented with a liquid perfume discovered by the Italian Count Frangipani who added alcohol to solid perfumes.
French Cloak	Long cloak cut either circular or semi-circular with a flat collar or shoulder cape.
French Hood	Worn mainly from 1521–1590. It was a small bonnet with a stiff base, the front curving on either side, covering the ears and worn back on the head. The edges were ornamented with billiments, and hanging down the back was a pleated or stiffened piece of material which could be turned back and worn over the crown, extending over the head and known as the Bongrace. Queen Mary (1553–1558) wore a variation of this with the crown flat and wide at the sides, folding back to cover the ears. It was fastened under the chin.
Frontlet	Decorative loop of silk or velvet suspended over the forehead worn with head attire.
Gabardine	Long, loose, wide-sleeved overcoat, worn with or without a girdle.
Gable Headdress	Another name for English hood, the front being shaped like a gable.
Head-rail	Square kerchief folded diagonally, worn as a shawl around the back of the head, becoming more elaborate in the second part of the century.
Jerkin	Type of cote-hardie, or jacket worn over a doublet, but with longer skirts. Could be either sleeveless with just wings, or with hanging sleeves.
	Ground-length chemise or petticoat made of silks, velvets, satin or taffeta, worn mainly as an under garment, beneath the gown. A kirtle consisted of a bodice and skirt.

Lappets	Plain or lace pendants hanging either from the sides or back of a head–dress.
Lettice Cap	Triangular shaped cap or bonnet, rising at the crown and covered the ears. Lettice was a grey fur similar to ermine.
Mandillion	Hip length jacket with side seams open, and close sleeves. Worn sideways fashionably.
Medici Collar	Lace or net collar standing up round the back of neck and sloping down on the front of the bodice.
Monmouth Cap	Tall, crowned, brimless, knitted cap.
Netherstocks	Lower part of hose.
Nightrail	Waistlength cape worn at night.
Palisadoe	Wire frame for raising the hair.
Panes	Ornamental parallel slits or slashes allowing the linings of contrasting colours to be pulled through them. They could also be ribbons joined together at either end.
Pantoffle	Common type of overshoe without a back, the front leather part similar to a mule. Eventually the name was also used for house shoes.
Partlet	Cover for a low necked décolletage which was either embroidered or decorated with jewels. It was similar to an under bodice or neckerchief.
Pattens	Wooden overshoes fastened by leather straps over boots or shoes, raising them above the dirty roads.
Peascod Body	Doublet padded in the front to the waist forming a bulge over the girdle.
Petticoat	Under-garment worn under a gown or by itself and tied to the dress by points. For male attire it was a padded under-doublet worn for extra warmth.
Pickadils	Tabbed or scalloped border on doublets in the early sixteenth century and in the late sixteenth century to *c.*1630 it became a tabbed or castellated support for collars.
Plackard	Stomacher or front piece to fill in the gap left by a V or U shaped opening in front. It could be embroidered or fur trimmed.
Pluderhose	Type of trunk hose, paned with wide gaps from which emerged masses of silk linings overhanging the panes. Mainly worn in the second half of the sixteenth century.
Points	Cords or laces with decorative metal tips used for joining hose etc. to breeches or separate sleeves to armholes. Also used as a form of decoration in groups and bows on garments.
Pomander	English name for the French *pomme d'ambre*. This could be an apple-shaped or flat container made in a filigree design to hold perfume. It could be worn on a chain around the neck or on a girdle, or could be carried in the hand.

Rebato	Collar wired to stand up around a low-necked bodice.
Roll Farthingale	Also known as a 'bum roll'. Consisting of a padded roll, sometimes wired, tied in the front with tapes. It was worn to distend the hips and tilted up slightly at the back and flattened towards the front.
Ruff	Circular collar, stiffly starched and gathered, radiating from the neck.
Slashings	Slits cut in various garments in a symmetrical design, allowing the lining to be pulled through in puffs.
Slops	Wide knee breeches.
Spanish Cloak	Short hooded cloak. The decorated hood was deep and pointed, whilst the cloak itself was full with a small turned-down collar. Popular 1535–1620.
Spanish Farthingale	Undergarment made with hoops of wicker, wood, wire or whalebone. They were so placed to give a funnel-shaped skirt. The petticoats were generally made of fustian or a heavy material, whilst the wealthier classes wore them made of silks or velvet.
Stomacher	Ornamental front piece to cover a low bodice or V or U fronted doublet.
Supportasse	Wire frame to support the large fashionable ruffs, sometimes covered with metal or coloured thread.
Taffeta Pipkin	Small, flat crowned hat, drawn in and pleated to a flat, narrow brim. Often decorated with a jewelled hat band and feather.
Tippet	Elongated tip of hood. Hanging streamers from sleeves. Short shoulder cape. Scarf, similar to a stole.
Trunk Hose	Short distended breeches joined to stockings or tights and attached to the doublet by points. From about 1560 they could be paned, revealing the padded lining which was of contrasting silks.
Trunk Hose	Upper part of leg-wear. Distended breeches, paned from c.1560, disclosing the contrasting linings. Attached to the stockings by points or lacing.
Trunk Sleeves	Sleeves tight to the wrist with the upper part wider and padded.
Underpropper	Another name for supportasse.
Upperstosks	Breeches or seat part of hose.
Vandyke	Term meaning notched or indented edging either of lace or material.
Venetian Breeches	Usually bombasted, pear-shaped breeches narrowing towards the knees. Most popular in the 1580s.
Wings	Stiff decorative crescent-shaped bands extending over the shoulder seams. When detachable sleeves were worn the wings hid the ties.

Select Bibliography

Asser, Joyce, *Historic Hairdressing*, Pitman 1966

Barfoot, A., *Everyday Costume in England*, Batsford 1961

Boehn, Max von, *Modes & Manners* (8 vols), Harrap 1926

Boucher, F., *History of Costume in the West*, Thames & Hudson 1967

Boucher, F., *20,000 Years of Fashion*, Abrams

Bradfield, N., *Historical Costumes of England*, Harrap 1958

Brooke, Iris, *English Costume in the Age of Elizabeth*, A. & C. Black 1964

Brooke, Iris, *History of English Costume*, Methuen 1937

Brooke, Iris, *Western European Costume*, Theatre Arts Books 1963

Calthorp, D.C., *English Costume*, A. & C. Black, 1906

Cooke, P.C., *English Costume*, Gallery Press, 1968

Courtais, G. de, *Women's Headdress & Hairstyles*, Batsford 1973

Cunnington, P., *Costume in Pictures*, Studio Vista 1964

Cunnington, C.W. and P., *Dictionary of English Costume 900–1900*, A. & C. Black 1972

Cunnington, C.W. and P., *Handbook of English Costume in the 16th Century*, Faber & Faber 1954

Davenport, Millia, *The Book of Costume*, Bonanza 1968

Francoise, Lejeune, *Histoire du Costume*, Editions Delalain

Garland, M., *The Changing Face of Beauty*, Weidenfeld & Nicholson 1957

Garland, M., *History of Fashion*, Orbis 1975

Gorsline, D., *What People Wore*, Bonanza 1951

Kelly, Mary, *On English Costume*, Deane 1934

Hansen, H., *Costume Cavalcade*, Methuen 1956

Hartnell, Norman, *Royal Courts of Fashion*, Cassell 1971

Koehler, C., *History of Costume*, Constable 1963

Laver, James, *Concise History of Costume*, Thames & Hudson 1963

Laver, James, *Costume*, Batsford 1956

Laver, James, *Costume Through the Ages*, Thames & Hudson 1964

Lister, Margot, *Costume*, Herbert Jenkins 1964

Norris, Herbert, *Costume & Fashion*, J.M. Dent 1924–38

Pistolese & Horstig, *History of Fashions*, Wiley 1970

Rupert, J., *Le Costume*, Flammarion 1930

Saint-Laurent, Cecil, *History of Ladies' Underwear*, Michael Joseph 1968

Truman, N., *Historic Costuming*, Pitman 1936

Wilcox, R.T., *Dictionary of Costume*, Batsford 1970

Wilson, E., *History of Shoe Fashion*, Pitman 1969

Yarwood, D., *English Costume from the Second Century BC to 1972*, Batsford 1972

Yarwood, D., *Outline of English Costume*, Batsford 1972

Pictorial Encyclopedia of Fashion, Hamlyn 1968

Index